ENDORSEMENTS

Most of the world thinks creating a business online is putting out a bunch of noise and hoping somebody listens. It's not. Jared & Kimanzi show you how to create a successful business, develop winning relationships, and serve your community for the long, long term.

AMY ROBLES
Think Enriched

I love to learn from those who are doing what they teach. Kimanzi Constable and Jared Easley live the words in this book. I highly recommend this book to anyone wanting a practical guide on how to grow a business the right way.

JIMMY BURGESS
#1 Best-selling author and speaker

In today's fast-paced online world, it may seem like connecting with big-name influencers is the only way to get noticed. Kimanzi and Jared show you a better way. This book will make you rethink how you build your business.

JODY MABERRY
Host of *Creating Disney Magic* Podcast

Take a bow!

STOP
CHASING
INFLUENCERS

PROV.
3:5-6

STOP
CHASING
INFLUENCERS

THE TRUE PATH TO
BUILDING YOUR BUSINESS
AND LIVING YOUR DREAM

KIMANZI CONSTABLE
JARED EASLEY

For more information on foreign distribution, call 717-530-2122.

Reach us on the Internet: www.soundwisdom.com.

Cover design by Eileen Rockwell

Sound Wisdom
P.O. Box 310
Shippensburg, PA 17257-0310

ISBN 13 TP: 978-0-7684-0893-5
ISBN 13 Ebook: 978-0-7684-0894-2

For Worldwide Distribution, Printed in the U.S.A.

1 2 3 4 5 6 7 8 / 18 17 16 15

CONTENTS

INTRODUCTION

If you're like us, you probably look up to and learn from many heroes. It's probably a dream to connect with those heroes who have influenced your life and business.

When you're starting out or trying to build your business, you may have considered what we call the "influencer shout-out strategy." You're told to try and connect with those at the top of your industry through sharing their content, commenting on their websites, and e-mailing them with the hope that they will respond to you and you can form relationships with them.

Once the relationship is established, you show them what you're doing with your business, hoping they will promote it to their large audience. You're told that you have to be persistent and add value to get them to connect with you.

On the surface, this all sounds like a good strategy, but it's not the best way to build your business.

This strategy may be popular, and there are different variations of it, but it's taking time away from better strategies that can help you build your business. Connecting with influencers is not what it used to be.

Influencers are busy; and since the publication of *The 4-Hour Workweek* by Timothy Ferriss, they're taking a step back. Sure, you can see them at events and even take pictures, but that connection only exists in your mind.

We're not trying to be harsh, but if you're going to get the kind of help you need, we have to be honest. Everyday people are trying the influencer shout-out strategy only to be disappointed.

Stop Chasing Influencers walks you through why and how you can become an influencer. Hint: it's not the money. We'll talk about what used to work, and give you a better strategy to build your business. We will end with how-to leverage opportunities.

By the end of this book, you will know what it takes to build a business in this crowded market without the help of an influencer.

As we write today, there are 900 million websites and 250 million blogs on the Internet, and 175,000 are added every day, according to Jeff Bullas, a leading digital marketing expert (http://www.jeffbullas.com/2014/04/03/5-steps-to-a-damn-good-content-marketing-strategy/). There are about 175,000 podcasts. To say there's a lot of competition is an understatement.

Because you're reading this, I'm guessing you've been on this business-building journey and are frustrated. In your frustration, you turn to what you've heard works. You've studied the field and done some research, and you probably have a wicked case of information overload.

There's a lot of information out there, but in this book we want to help you figure out what works. We know you're busy, so we don't want to waste your time. We will get straight to the point.

Building your dream on the side is hard. You have a day job and a family. You have other responsibilities alongside the general craziness of life. Finding time to build your dream seems impossible.

It's a dilemma because you don't have time, but if you don't make the time, your dream will never happen. Kimanzi remembers experiencing this dilemma clearly when he was building his business.

He worked fifty to sixty hours a week delivering bread. He had a wife and three growing children, and had responsibilities at church. He slept three to five hours a night for twelve years, but still dreamed of being a writer.

Despite all the craziness, he found time to write two books, create several products, speak all around the world, and build an online business that supports his family.

It might seem like a lot, but it wasn't half as much as he could have accomplished if he'd been focused. He could have done a lot more, and gotten here faster, with two major tips.

If you're chasing a dream on the side, you're going to have to use every minute wisely. You can make your dream happen a lot quicker with two simple tips: 1) cutting out the distractions, and 2) focusing on what is most important.

CUT OUT THE DISTRACTIONS

As you're reading this, you're probably thinking, "Duh," but how many tabs do you have open right now on your computer? Are your e-mail and social media notifications turned on? Are you getting calls that really aren't that important while you're trying to work?

Every minute is precious, and when you use those minutes catering to distractions, that's one less minute you can spend on your dream. Those little distractions are time killers, and if you added up the time, you would be shocked.

Dan Miller is a multimillionaire and *New York Times* best-selling author of *48 Days to the Work You Love*. Last year he held a challenge to create one new product every month. Not only did he create those products, he wrote a new book on top of it! He also reads one book a week.

Read that paragraph over again and say, "Wow!"

One thing we've heard Dan say over and over is that he works in uninterrupted blocks of time. He eliminates the distractions, especially the ones just mentioned. He uses that time to focus and work.

Can we all be superstars like Dan Miller? One hundred percent *yes!* You may not get as much accomplished in the same amount of time, but you can get more accomplished than you ever thought possible.

Kimanzi just interviewed Stacy Claffin. She wakes up every day at 4:00 a.m. and writes until 7:00 A.M. During those three hours she cuts out all other distractions. Working without distractions has allowed her to write and release eleven books since November 2012. Did we mention that she has two kids whom she homeschools, and also runs a day care?

This is how you create rock-star content that grows your audience, changes lives, and brings hope to the world. Social media will come and go, but your dream can change your life and give you true freedom.

Look, we all have different things going on in our lives. You may not have huge blocks of time to work on your dream. The point is to use whatever you have, and to do the best you can.

ONE-DAY TEST

We challenge you to work an uninterrupted block of time for one day. When you sit down to work on your dream, turn everything else off. At the end of that time period, see what you've accomplished compared to what you normally do. If it works, you might want to continue and build until it's a habit that helps you create and grow your dream!

FOCUS ON WHAT IS MOST IMPORTANT RIGHT NOW

How many blogs do you read every day? How many podcasts do you listen to? There's a ton of information out there and it's easy to get information overload. As a matter of fact, most people starting out or people who haven't seen progress end up getting information overload.

Jason Van Orden and Jeremy Frandsen from Internet Business Mastery introduced the idea of "just-in-time learning." Just-in-time learning is about "only consuming the information that immediately applies to what you need to do next, what you want to accomplish next in your business" (http://www .internetbusinessmastery.com/transcripts-ibm-107-how-to-end -the-overwhelm-in-internet-business/).

We want answers, and we want our business to be built better and faster. In our effort to do that, we turn to information. Information overload has crippled many a dream, and there's an easy fix: *focus on what's most important right now.*

If you're just starting out, your focus should be on creating amazing content and building your e-mail list. That's where your focus should be, not on reading an article about affiliate marketing tips. Not on listening to a podcast about SEO tactics.

Too often we see an A-lister do something cool that generated a bunch of money, and we want to try it. We download the plugin; we install that widget. We buy that program, and in the end it's a complete waste of time. We spend hours just trying to figure out how to use the thing, and that's precious time that could be used building our audience one person at a time.

That's where they are at in their journey, not where you should try to be. Instead, you need to do what's going to make progress where you are. The thing that always makes progress and actually builds your business is making lifelong customers. Let's say it again because this point is so critical. *The thing that always makes progress and actually builds your business is making lifelong customers.*

That's the advantage you have when you're "small"—you can make a personal connection with every new audience member. That personal connection is what makes lifelong customers.

Don't run down the rabbit holes. Instead, focus on what you need to work on where you are in the journey. Do that, and then move on to all those cool things. Realize that in the end, good content is what people are looking for. All the fancy plug-ins and widgets are nice, but if the content doesn't back it up, people aren't coming back. Have you ever gone back to a restaurant that looked good but had yucky food?

Look, you can build a business that supports your family if you have the right focus, cut out the distractions, and hustle. We can tell you from personal experience that this life is better than you can imagine.

There's nothing like having the freedom to spend time on the things that are important to you. To live life on your terms, not the system's. This book is here to help you live that life of freedom. The difference is to create this life on your own. It's hard, but you can do it.

Tania Dakka is the founder of the Garage Party. Tania does a good job with writing persuasive sales copy. However, being great at something and getting clients to pay for this skill are two different things. Tania understood that the best way to grow her business was to connect with as many of her ideal clients as possible.

She did not have a large e-mail list, and she did not have a big platform online, but that did not stop her from being creative and trying something different. She was able to identify her avatar and develop a strategy to connect, despite not having the other things that most people assume are needed to grow a successful business.

What Tania did is simple but powerful. I do not want you to miss this if you are using a highlighter or taking notes. Tania focused on *what she had*, rather than what she was missing. She took inventory and realized that her assets at that time were her social media channels. She had a passion for music. She had a desire to generously connect. This was more than enough to start the Garage Party!

The Garage Party strategy is smart for multiple reasons. Tania identified her target clients and offered to highlight them during a Friday night "Garage Party" on social media. Tania started featuring her ideal customers (targeted entrepreneurs) by sharing a little bit about their business as well as their favorite songs on her social media channels.

She reached out to these customers beforehand to get their permission, and all were happy to be featured. Tania received great feedback from doing this. The Garage Party was born.

Tania gave shout-outs to her target clients on her social media channels, and it allowed her to connect with *hundreds* of her target customers. The Garage Party helped the featured entrepreneurs to sell more books, sell plug-ins, and make valuable connections with other networks as well.

Tania generated an incredible amount of goodwill by doing this. The entrepreneurs featured on the Garage Party shared the posts to their networks and recommended other entrepreneurs to be featured in following weeks.

You can probably guess the outcome of this simple idea. Tania's network continues to grow every week, and she continues to get new business by helping her target clients with the sales copy written on their websites.

Tania also takes the list of featured entrepreneurs from the Garage Party and adds them to her blog every Monday morning in a post called the "Monday Morning Mosh Pit." The blog post ends up getting shared and provides links to the featured entrepreneurs' websites. Jared was fortunate to interview Tania about the Garage Party on *Starve the Doubts* (http://www .starvethedoubts.com/108-tania-dakka-garage-party/).

If you think Tania's idea for the Garage Party is interesting, please send a tweet to @taniadakka, @jaredeasley, and @kimanzic and use the hashtag #garagepartyidea.

The rest of this book will outline various ideas and strategies that will help you leverage your existing assets and begin to grow your business. Please consider asking yourself what assets you have right now that may not seem obvious.

What could you do with these assets to grow your network and provide value to your target audience? What impact could that have on growing your business? If you have questions, feel free to reach out to us at www.stopchasinginfluencers.com. You can also find all the bonus material from the book there.

PART ONE

THE WHY

CHAPTER 1

FREEDOM

At the end of the day, the reason you're building a business is because you want freedom. You want to live life on your terms and spend it doing what's important to you. You're probably building this business on the side trying to leave a day job.

Jared and I talk to people every day who want to make a move from their day job to their dream job. If you're on the fence about whether you want to leave that day job, think about this: every week people all around the world spend forty hours plus at a job they absolutely hate. According to the *Washington Post*, only 13 percent of people are at a job they can tolerate. We don't have to give you the stats because chances are you are in a job you can't stand (http://www.washingtonpost.com/blogs/on-leadership/wp/2013/10/10/only-13-percent-of-people-worldwide-actually-like-going-to-work/).

Kimanzi worked a job he hated for twelve years. Every day his hatred for the job grew. When he started this job at nineteen years of age everything was fine. He was young and had the energy of a bull. OK, that might be an exaggeration, but he could handle the long hours. Once he was married with kids, the long hours started to wear on him.

It got even worse when Kimanzi's kids started participating in activities at school. He started this job at midnight, which meant on those nights he would get three hours of sleep.

Sleeping three hours a night and working sixty hours a week sucked, but what Kimanzi didn't realize was the effect it had on his health and the rest of his life. It was so bad that after he quit this job, he needed a month to detox.

We know there are many people reading this who can relate. Every day you go to a job that makes you miserable, wondering if you'll ever escape. What you may not be thinking about is how this job is affecting your life.

THE STRESS IS AFFECTING YOUR HEALTH

Stress is the leading cause of many health problems. An article titled "10 Health Problems Related to Stress That You Can Fix" on WebMD.com points out at least ten of them (http://www
.webmd.com/balance/stress-management/features/10-fixable
-stress-related-health-problems). When you spend day in and day out at a job you hate, you'd better believe you will be stressed out.

Over years that stress adds up, and you could end up with the health problems laid out in this article. Whether or not you realize it, you bring that stress home with you, and it affects everyone around you.

Years of stress could shorten your life and make you a bitter person. The longer you deal with stress, the more problems it leads to. One of the best things you can do is avoid stressful situations as much as possible. That's one reason why Kimanzi doesn't talk about politics on Facebook!

It's Fostering Bad Habits

Besides the stress, working at a job you hate can foster other bad habits. One major problem is sleeping issues. As mentioned, the odd hours Kimanzi worked had him sleeping three hours a night for years.

You may be getting more than three hours, but if you're at a job you hate, you're probably either getting too much or not enough.

You might also develop bad eating habits, be quick to anger, zone out, or notice a host of other problems. When you're at a job you hate, you turn to an outlet—an escape—and often it's not a healthy one.

It's Making You Complacent

If you stay at a job you hate for years, you could be training yourself to accept mediocrity. That may sound a little extreme, but think about it. You're learning how to settle for a "good enough" situation, and that will affect how you think about other situations in your life. When you start to settle in life, you're heading down a slippery slope. Time is the only resource we'll never get back. If you settle, you're wasting that precious time on something you'll regret later.

Whenever we think about breaking away from complacency, we think of the following amazing Steve Jobs quote:

> Here's to the crazy ones. The misfits. The rebels. The troublemakers. The round pegs in the square holes. The ones who see things differently. They're not fond of rules. And they have no respect for the status quo. You can quote them, disagree with them, glorify or vilify them. About the only thing you can't do is ignore them. Because they change things. They push the human race forward. And while some may

21

see them as the crazy ones, we see genius. Because the people who are crazy enough to think they can change the world, are the ones who do. ("Think different" was an advertising slogan for Apple, Inc., then Apple Computer, Inc., in 1997 created by the Los Angeles office of advertising agency TBWA\Chiat\Day.)

It's Affecting Other Areas of Your Life

The stress, bad habits, and complacency will not stay at work; you will bring them home with you. For a long time we thought we could separate work life and home life. We thought we could be miserable for ten hours a day, get done with work, and then go home and forget about it. It took awhile, but we realized that what happens to you for those hours will affect your home.

You're bringing all that junk with you. You might not be screaming and kicking chairs over, but when you're quiet and moody, your family notices. They can pick up on your tension, and it makes them tense. They won't know how to deal with you.

It's Keeping You from the Life You Truly Deserve

At the end of the day, a job you hate is sucking the life out of you. It's making you miserable, stressing you out, and affecting other areas of your life. It's keeping you from an existence you truly deserve.

There's an amazing life waiting if you're willing to do something about it. We're not telling you this will be easy. Life isn't a movie where everything magically works out. What we are telling you is that if you're willing to do what it takes, you can leave a job you hate. Realize that this takes time.

We know what you're thinking because we hear it all the time, "Good for them." No, it's not just good for us; it's good for many who decided they wanted more.

Determine right now that every time you fall, you'll get back up. In the end, to create this amazing life, perseverance has to be your best friend. The clock is ticking. The reason we do this is to create businesses that support a life we love.

Joseph Michael wanted to create a business that supported a life he would love. He was actively blogging as a side hustle to his day job. Joseph has an amazing wife and two beautiful daughters. He knew he could not leave his day job to become a full-time blogger.

Joseph needed a plan. He knew some of the struggles that writers and bloggers face because he was in the trenches doing the work as well. He had his "aha" moment not long after he learned about Scrivener, a writing software.

Joseph noticed some blog comments that referenced Scrivener's interface and opportunities to help writers. He also noticed that while the Scrivener tool was valuable, it was not easy to learn. The tool was great, but there was no training available.

Blog commenters agreed. They complimented the tool, but identified the pain that writers experience when they first attempt to learn it. Joseph noticed a comment from *The New York Times* best-selling author Michael Hyatt that stated he wished he could pay for a tutorial that would help him quickly learn to use Scrivener.

Joseph knew exactly what to do! He jumped on the opportunity and started working on Learn Scrivener Fast, a series of video tutorials that helped writers use and benefit from the Scrivener writing tool in almost no time at all.

The story gets better!

Joseph did not have a large platform or influence among fellow writers who would benefit from his new program, but this did not stop or deter him. He connected with other writers who had large e-mail lists, and leveraged affiliate opportunities that allowed him to cohost webinars for larger audiences. The webinars not only provided great value to writers; they also converted to sales for his new program! The content piece from the webinar, combined with an offering to purchase the Learn Scrivener Fast program, was a huge hit!

Joseph was able to get in front of larger audiences, provide great information on webinars, and convert them to sales that he would not have made using his own limited marketing efforts. He continued this process for several months and made enough money to prove to himself that he was ready to turn pro and leave his day job behind.

He had increased savings, which made his wife and him feel more stable, and he prepared to go from working a full-time job to being a full-time entrepreneur. Joseph wanted freedom in his life, and he created an opportunity to make that freedom his reality.

We are building these businesses to have the freedom to spend our time doing what's important to us. Life is too short to live any other way.

If you want to achieve true freedom, you have to beat any self-limiting beliefs. For too many of us, we want to be the "rock"—we don't want anyone to think we have any weakness. This means we keep our problems and struggles to ourselves. We even keep them from those we love. We want to be strong, but at the end of the day we're human. We go through highs and lows, and struggle with self-limiting beliefs. We tell ourselves things that hold us back from being the best men and women we could be.

These things may not be verbalized, and we might not even be aware of them, but there are ten things we have to stop telling ourselves if we want to live an amazing life. These self-limiting beliefs are affecting us one way or another. They're paralyzing us and keeping too many of us from even thinking about taking action on our dream lifestyle. They're keeping us in toxic relationships; they're keeping us at jobs we hate; they're keeping us from moving to somewhere better; and they're keeping us from being the best we can be.

We have listened to them for far too long. It's time to get real with ourselves and to stop settling in life. We only get one life to live, and these self-limiting beliefs are keeping us from truly living it. Here are ten lies we tell ourselves that hold us back:

1. I'm not good-looking

You may not look like a celebrity, but you don't have to. You're good-looking, and you need to know that. Confidence is an attractive quality, and there is someone out there for all of us. Don't listen to anyone who tells you otherwise. They're wrong.

2. I'm not smart enough

Sure, not all of us are Albert Einstein, but we don't have to be. You may not be book smart, but you might be street smart. You may not have gone to Harvard, but you did get a degree from a state college. You may not have gone to college, but as long as you commit to always learn, you are as smart as you need to be. At the Expert's Academy live event, Kimanzi heard Brendon Burchard say, "An expert is a student first." Always continue to learn and better educate yourself about the things you need to know.

3. I can't beat my fear

The fear of failure keeps too many of us feeling stuck. We're afraid to even try because we think we'll fail. Fear is a liar and a dream killer. You can't let it win. C JoyBell C made a great observation about fear: "Don't be afraid of your fears. They're not there to scare you. They're there to let you know that something is worth it" (C JoyBell C in *Saint Paul Trois Chateaux*).

4. I live a good enough life

You could go through life taking the safe road every time, but how boring is that? Life is too short to settle, and you only get one chance to live it. Don't let fear keep you from true freedom and living on your terms. The following is just a line from the movie *Braveheart*, but the words are true and powerful: "Why? Why is that impossible? You're so concerned with squabbling for the scraps from Longshanks' table that you've missed your God-given right to something better."

5. What other people are saying is true

Negative people will try to hold you back in life. They could be outright haters or just people who aren't comfortable in their own lives. These people will point out the hundred reasons you'll never succeed. Don't listen to them; cut them out of your life if you have to.

6. It's too hard so i won't try

Making big changes isn't easy, but once you reach your goal, it will be totally worth the struggle. Change is hard, just like life. There's no easy road for most of us, but that's OK. The struggle teaches us to appreciate what we have once we get it. Even though it's hard, try anyway. That's how you learn and grow.

7. I don't deserve happiness

Difficult life situations, or decisions we've made in the past may have planted the seed in our minds that we don't deserve happiness. That is a straight-up lie. No matter who you are or where you're at in life, you deserve to be happy. More than that, you can be happy if you choose to be happy.

8. It will never work out for me

It may seem as though everyone around you has an amazing life with no problems, but that's just a front. We all have struggles, and it often feels as though nothing will ever work out the way we want it to. That's just a feeling that can be overcome with a mind-set shift.

9. No one understands what i'm going through

What you're going through may be difficult, but we guarantee there's some other person going through the same thing. It's hard to open up and communicate, but keeping all those emotions bottled up inside could negatively affect your health. There is someone who understands, and there are great benefits in getting through it together.

10. This is as good as it gets

The quality of your life comes down to what you decide you want it to be. If you decide it will never get better, you won't take the necessary steps to make it better. Stop letting self-limiting beliefs keep you stuck in a life you hate. Decide that today is the day you're going to reclaim your existence. Don't listen to doubt, fear, or the negative voices of others. Make the decision that even though it's not easy, you're going to do what it takes to create an amazing life. You're going to live a life most people only dream of living.

Don't get me wrong—truly living an amazing existence is hard work. It's takes time and more perseverance than we think we have in us, but nothing is impossible. Decide that today is the day you're going to reclaim your life. Make that decision, but do something different. Take action.

ARE YOU LETTING SELF-LIMITING BELIEFS HOLD YOU BACK?

Freedom starts with liberating your mind and realizing your dream is possible. We know things may not have gone as planned. We know this is frustrating, but freedom is possible for you. And you can do it on your *own!*

Chapter 2

SERVING THOSE WHO NEED YOUR HELP

Your *why* goes beyond freedom. You do this to help people. You may be training on a wide range of topics, but you're training to help people through some of their biggest struggles.

If you're not coming at this from a place of service, you're in the wrong business. Let us paint a picture of what the world of Internet marketing looks like today.

You've seen it. Right? The courses from the big Internet marketers telling you about their seven-figure system. You've seen countless testimonials from people who have used these courses and are now millionaires. The websites look good; the copy on the sales pages is very convincing. You're frustrated that you haven't seen results, so you start working out ways to afford the course.

You think about it. You may have even talked it over with your spouse. You go back to the sales page, but something in your gut is gnawing at you. We have to tell you that you should be grateful for whatever is keeping you from buying.

Don't get us wrong. There are many great products out there from some amazing entrepreneurs. However, there are just as many that promise results but deliver disappointment.

BUYER BEWARE

In our online business journey we've spent over $8,000 on courses that promised big results. In the end, the courses didn't help our business—daily hustle and basic marketing principles did.

There are problems in the Internet marketing world today that unfortunately many people are falling victim to. Before you buy a product or service, we want you to think about the following:

A lot of the advice only works if you have a huge audience.

This is the biggest problem in Internet marketing today. There's a ton of great advice that will only work once your online presence reaches a certain point. The reason big Internet marketers do so well is because of their affiliates. A big online presence means a business has a lot of affiliates willing to promote its products and services.

A lot of the information available gives you a great plan but neglects the most important part of building an online business: *building your audience.* Most Internet marketing programs don't teach you how to get more traffic and e-mail subscribers. That's because they didn't build their online businesses in a time like ours, where there's a ton of competition.

Our advice is to save your money and focus on building traffic and e-mail subscribers. That's what builds your business to the point that it can support your family.

The courses are designed to get you to buy more.

A lot of the courses from big Internet marketers are designed to upsell you on something more expensive. Remember, Kimanzi went to two high-end Internet marketing events and has seen the back end of all of this.

You buy the $97 program, and before you can check out, you're taken to a page offering you 50 percent off the $2,000 program, and it's ten times better than the one you're thinking about buying.

Impulse kicks in, and you don't want to miss out on the "deal," so you upgrade. Even if you don't, you take the $97 program and are left missing the valuable information you need to grow your business.

That's how these big courses are designed. When you're creating your own programs, run away from this model. If you give your customers unbelievable value, you won't have to trick them into buying something else.

The results are often inflated.

When you look at the seven-figure launch claims, you have to break down that number. Yes, it may have been a seven-figure launch, but what are the expenses? What does this business have to pay its affiliates? What other events were thrown in for free to get you to buy?

In the online world it's easy to lie, and a lot of people do it. They lie to impress you and convince you that buying their stuff is a good investment. If you want to know the truth, you have to talk to current and past customers.

If you look at the testimonials for a lot of big courses, you aren't able to contact those customers. The first thing we tell anyone who's interested in working with us is to feel free to contact anyone we've worked with. Their names and websites are right on our coaching pages. That's how it should be with your business. Go out of your way to let people see the real you and the real results your clients are getting. If your clients aren't getting results, you know you have work to do.

You can't get the personal help you need.

Many courses are video-based. You watch six videos, maybe get a PDF, and that's it. Those videos could be the six greatest videos you've ever watched in your life, but as you try to implement the principles, we guarantee you'll have questions.

Those questions won't be answered because all that is offered is the videos. If you're going to buy a program or course, make sure there are live office hours so you can get specific questions answered.

The person who's building can't afford it.

At the end of the day, most of us can't afford expensive programs and courses. We have families, mortgages, cars, and the normal expenses of life. While we advocate spending money to improve yourself and your business, you have to be realistic about where those dollars are spent.

Often money is spent in the frustration of our current progress. You end up hating your dream because you don't make progress, and now you're in debt. You have to be realistic about what you can afford, but more than that, what will help you *where you are*. You don't have a bunch of affiliates; you aren't building a niche site; and you aren't creating a membership program. Most of us are just trying to make our first $1,000. We've talked to many who have made a hundred dollars but haven't crossed that $1,000 mark yet. If that's you, these big courses won't help you.

REMEMBER: THIS ISN'T ABOUT NUMBERS.

When you start your entrepreneurial journey, you want to build your numbers. Whether it's your social media presence, e-mail list, or visibility, you associate a larger number with growth.

Larger numbers, however, aren't as important as you think. Just because an entrepreneur has large numbers online doesn't mean it has translated into income for his or her business.

Here are several reasons why entrepreneurs—especially online—need to look beyond the numbers and focus on what builds a business.

The numbers don't indicate engagement.

Your business won't grow if you have a large social media presence, a large e-mail list, or a lot of people visiting your website but zero engagement. The best leads are word-of-mouth leads, and those come through the engagement of your fans and followers. If your online presence is a ghost town, large numbers won't help your business.

Your goal should be to engage your audience. Get them involved in the conversation in such a way that they want to share it with others. Your community should be so engaged that your reach goes far beyond your numbers.

Personal connection is what creates lifelong customers.

Several years ago, *New York Times* best seller *The 4-Hour Workweek* was all the rage. The book talked about automating your business to the point of being hands off. While the concept of this book is entertaining and can work for a certain type of entrepreneur, the reality is that in order for you to create lifelong customers, you have to establish a personal connection.

People buy from someone they know, like, and trust, and that will never happen communicating through a virtual assistant. A customer is a person, and the more he or she gets that personal connection, the more that customer will buy and the more he or she will tell others about your business. Marketing genius David Ogilvy said in his 1964 book, *Confessions of an Advertising Man*, "The consumer is not an idiot, she's your wife." Make that personal connection.

Numbers can easily be manipulated.

If you want a large following, it's pretty easy to buy one, and too many entrepreneurs today do just that. Every day, on social media and through e-mail, you see services offering fans for a price. The problem is that those aren't real people, and they will never buy from you. Big numbers may look impressive but they won't translate into income if they're not real people. You have to ask yourself if the numbers are more important than the income.

Your numbers will increase if you add value.

As you add value and connect in a personal way with your audience, engagement will increase. With an increase in engagement comes more people sharing your business, which will increase your numbers organically.

Great content, products, and services speak for themselves and create a loyal fan base that will spread the message all over the Internet. Over time your numbers will increase in the best way possible because all your new fans and followers will already be engaged.

BUILDING A BUSINESS IS NOT ABOUT EGO

Who doesn't like to look at their platform and see huge numbers? That said, we are in business to generate income and make an impact in people's lives. This isn't about numbers.

While it's great to have large numbers and it can be good social proof, your business can be successful with a small, devoted following. You can create lifelong customers who do all of your advertising for you. We have to focus on business, not our ego or our emotions.

We own a business in a time when the economy is recovering and there are many other businesses that do what we do. The good news is that some of the greatest businesses were built during downtimes.

If you want to be one of those businesses, you have to stand out from the competition by building a devoted customer base. Focus on creating amazing content. Focus on creating irresistible products and services. Focus on really connecting and engaging people. When you do, they will respond and your numbers will build. It's too easy to get caught up in the comparison game. That game will direct you down a road that derails your business from growing. Numbers are OK, but real people are better.

Look, we've been there. We were frustrated and wanted to make progress, and wanted to quit jobs that sucked the life out of us. We've tried a lot of things, but the thing that helped us the most was the daily hustle.

That hustle involves consistently posting great content on your blog, guest posting on sites that have a larger audience than yours, and going after interviews on podcasts where you can share your story. Build your e-mail list, connect with your audience, and create products and services that help your target audience.

It just takes time. Once you hustle, your eyes open to the opportunities around you, and you start to go for them. Instead of trying to be like all the big names, be the person in the shadows who focuses on helping those you serve.

CHAPTER 3

A LARGE PLATFORM TO SPREAD A MESSAGE

Each of us has a story and message that we want to spread to the world. If you're reading this you probably want to spread your message to the biggest audience possible.

Everyone's trying to build a platform these days. Bloggers. Speakers. Musicians. Everyone. The question is, once you have a platform, what will you do with it?

DON'T BE ANOTHER NOISEMAKER

There are a lot of people in this world trying to get heard. They are eager for an audience. Some, though, are going about it the wrong way. And they're paying dearly for it. These people have turned their channels into monologues. They've hijacked the conversation and made it about themselves. They need to get in touch with what earned them influence in the first place. They need to refocus on others.

We've all seen the importance of a platform and why you need one to get published. We understand how to earn the attention of an audience, so let's talk about what comes *after*. What do you do once you've *built* a platform? How do you continue connecting with people and spreading a message that deserves to be heard?

The following are three tips to remember:

1. Broadcast your passion.

With negativity surrounding us from all sides, we need something to motivate us. Something positive. Something that matters. Do you have this kind of message? If you don't, it might be time to rethink what you're spreading. What we need is your pathos, your *love*—not just another angry rant. The temptation to make a buck in the short term is alluring, as is the opportunity to be controversial. Eventually, though, people see through this approach. Why not try something radical instead? Start letting your passion be heard. Make it loud and clear. This resonates more than another piece of bad news.

2. Give back.

A great way to build a platform is to be generous—to give away something for free, like an e-book. Once you've done this, don't stop. There is always something more to give, always another way to share. Look for ways to help people.

Think of all the good you could be doing with your newfound influence. How about taking that guest post from an unknown writer? Or grabbing coffee with someone ready to learn? Take what you've received and pay it forward. Don't resent the attention you receive—*embrace* it. As much as you can, even if it takes a while, *answer* those requests for advice. Reply to e-mails asking for help. Don't get cocky, remember how you got here, and don't forget to give back.

3. Make your message matter.

Do you know what it's going to take to make an impact in this world? You and me and the messages we're spreading, dripped out over time to our audiences. What we think and write every day. We're being heard on a regular basis. That's how you make a difference. And that's why you build a platform: to communicate in a way that changes things.

You could do all the right things to make your story spread, but if you don't put out a consistently important message, you're irrelevant. Just another noisemaker in an already noisy world. So keep showing up. Keep sharing a message worth hearing.

As Seth Godin says, we need you to lead us. So start leading. And do so generously. We're all waiting to hear from you.

Why do you want to build a platform? Is it to help people? Or to self-promote? Don't be one of those people who get to the top and scream messages that don't matter. Focus on coming from a place of service. Focus on helping people with the problems you've progressed through.

GO BIG BY GOING SMALLER

Jonathan Harrison was going through the motions and doing what seemed to be right. His leadership blog was great, but it was not getting much traction despite his consistency. His posts were creative and addressed relevant matters for aspiring leaders, but Google analytics responded with mostly crickets and tumbleweeds. I love what happened next.

A lot of people would have been discouraged and possibly given up. However, Jonathan is not like everyone else. Jonathan took a barometer check at the beginning of the year. He realized that his topic was great, but it was too broad. He examined what he could do differently. He asked himself what his unfair advantage was and something he would enjoy writing about at the same time. He considered how he could add more of himself.

Jonathan had already tested some interesting ideas through his "Casual Friday" posts. He began to sneak in posts about video games primarily because it interested him. He realized after doing this a few times that this was the topic he really wanted to write about. Jonathan quickly narrowed his audience by being specific. He realized who to write to, and this gave him immense clarity. His blog *Classically Trained* was born! The new blog mashed together effective leadership and personal productivity solutions made accessible through video-game metaphors and analogies. The new posts were fun, engaging, and professional.

He created a blog post about time management techniques learned from the video game Tetris (http://classicallytrained.net/tetris-time-management/), and the article was shared on Twitter. It ended up being mentioned on *Lifehacker* (http://lifehacker.com/treat-your-e-mail-like-tetris-one-action-at-a-time-1550288250)! Can you imagine? Jonathan had tried for months with his previous blog to get this sort of opportunity, but it never came. *Lifehacker* was not Jonathan's only win. He was invited to speak at Florida Supercon in Miami, and asked to speak to the leadership team at the Boca Raton Regional Hospital. Jonathan has also been featured on CNN, contributed articles to *Fast Company*, and been quoted on Monster.com.

Imagine for a minute what could happen if your topic was narrowed and examined. What could happen if you could find your unfair advantage, which also happens to be something you enjoy as well.

Jonathan had some amazing wins once he developed immense clarity and realized to whom he was writing. The purpose of this book is to help you be like Jonathan. If you're going to be successful at spreading your message, build these fundamentals into your strategy.

If you were to study successful entrepreneurs, what you would find might surprise you. The things that make them successful aren't a mystery; there weren't any "silver bullets" that propelled them to success. Too often we're looking for that one tip or trick that's going to make all the difference in our business. The reality is that with a few simple tweaks of the "basics," we could be just as successful.

We live in a great time to be an entrepreneur, and there are many opportunities all around us. There are also many businesses doing the very same thing as we are.

BE DIFFERENT AND STAND OUT

To thrive today you can't conform and copy. To be successful you have to be different and stand out. *The following are some things to help you stand out, things that successful entrepreneurs do differently.*

They model, not copy.

When you're frustrated with the lack of progress and income in your business, you naturally look to those who are successful. You believe that if you copy what they're doing, you could get the results they're getting. Unfortunately it doesn't work that way.

When you're the carbon copy of someone else, people will do business with that person, not you. Model systems that work and use successful frameworks. Learn from the strategies that make them successful, but do it in a way that's unique to you and your business.

They're clear about who their customer is

Successful entrepreneurs serve a specific target market. They realize that you can't reach everyone, and if you try, your efforts will be ineffective and scattered. To grow your business, you have to spend your time and resources in the places that will get you the best results.

Chasing people who will probably never buy from you is not a great use of your time. Time is money for entrepreneurs; wasting it in the places that don't generate income is not what helps you become successful.

They don't rely too heavily on any one strategy.

Social media has been great for business, but it has become the crutch for too many entrepreneurs. Successful entrepreneurs have a very diverse strategy that doesn't rely too heavily on any one thing. They realize that at any time, what used to work might not anymore, so they leave room to pivot.

Case in point would be the algorithm changes for Google and Facebook. Some entrepreneurs folded because they relied too heavily on one strategy. The smart entrepreneurs moved on to plan B. Have multiple ways to market your business; have multiple streams of income; have an emergency fund and a back-up plan.

They keep it simple.

We live in a time when information is readily available. Every day we listen to podcasts, watch videos, and read blogs that give us amazing strategies to grow our business. The problem comes in the form of information overload.

We get stuck because we get confused on what we should be working on right now and what will lead to the best results. Successful entrepreneurs firmly believe in the speed of implementation. How fast can you take a good idea and create a product or service from that idea?

Successful entrepreneurs realize that perfection is a curse. Instead, they get their idea to market and improve upon it. They keep it simple by learning and then implementing.

Keep all aspects of your business lean and clean. From your website down to your social media profiles, don't confuse or frustrate people.

They don't let self-limiting beliefs stunt their business.

At some point in his or her journey, every successful entrepreneur has struggled with self-limiting beliefs. You will, too. These beliefs are things you're telling yourself that hinder the actions you take in your business. Examples of such beliefs include:

- Your content isn't good enough.

- You can't raise your prices.

- There's too much competition.

- You don't have enough credentials.

- You don't have enough resources.

Successful entrepreneurs have beaten these self-limiting beliefs and keep them from creeping back into their minds. If you're going to be successful at anything, it starts in your mind. Despite all the bad news about our economy, your business can thrive if you focus on things that create success. Here's to you and your businesses success.

MANY OF US WANT A LARGE PLATFORM TO SPREAD A MESSAGE OF HOPE.

Kimanzi and his friends had the privilege of coaching an inner-city teen basketball team this year. The team did well and made it all the way to the championship game. Coming into the tournament they felt pretty good about their chances. They were up seven games to one, then lost one game. After that, they beat teams by twenty to thirty points. Coming into the championship game they felt pretty good about the team and the players' abilities.

As the game went on, something weird started to happen. The team was not playing a normal game. The opposing team, which Kimanzi's players had beaten by twenty points the last time they'd played, was keeping up this time. In the fourth quarter the game was neck and neck. Three of Kimanzi's best players had four fouls and were in danger of fouling out of the game. At that moment Kimanzi and his friends, and even some of the players, were losing hope.

All those hidden doubts that existed coming into the game were screaming in their heads as their hope faded and doubt increased. Then, with thirty seconds or so left, the other team was winning by one point. The ball was inbounded and passed two times to Kimanzi's best player, and at that moment the hope started overtaking the doubt.

He got the ball and drove to the basket—it was like something out of a movie—and he made the shot as the time ran out. They won the championship!

When you're chasing your dreams, hope is the fuel in your gas tank. When you have no hope, you have no real chance of succeeding. With everything that's going on in our economy—in our world—we see a lack of hope. People are searching for it. You might be one of those people. *Do you have hope?* If you do, are you spreading the message of hope?

Hope Is Your Shield to Stop Doubt

Whether it's chasing your dreams, starting a dream job, or starting a business, you will always have doubts. Even when you see some success, your doubts will never go away. When you have doubts, hope can make them look silly.

There was no reason for Kimanzi and his friends to have doubt. Their team had been solid all year. The doubt only started to take over when they lost hope. If you have a step-by-step plan and have done the proper research, there's no need for you to listen to doubt. When you start facing doubt, you need hope. You should have hope based off your planning.

Hope Is Our Strength in Times of Despair

Have you ever talked to someone who just lost a job? Have you been part of a company that is going through layoffs? Have you seen a business that has to close down because of lack of customers? In all these situations the hope is gone, and it leads to depression and anger. What these people really need is hope.

How much of a difference is there when people who lost their jobs get a call to come in for a job interview? At that moment they snap out of those other emotions. They have hope of getting that job. When the company in the midst of layoffs has a great quarter, all of a sudden there's hope in that office. When people are going through the worst situations in their lives, hope can get them through those situations. They need this hope. We need this hope.

ARE YOU SPREADING THE MESSAGE OF HOPE?

Negative emotions can be contagious, but hope can be far more contagious. That's why we need to spread this message of hope. If you want to chase your dreams, there is hope for you. We are in the greatest time of opportunity. There is opportunity everywhere if you're willing to see it.

Hope seems so elusive if you watch or read the news. Every day there is a story that makes you doubt and lose hope. *Stop!* Ignore the news. Don't listen to the negative attitudes of other people. Hope is all around you, and your dreams deserve hope.

Life is too short for you to lose hope and not live the life you deserve. Hold on to hope and chase your dreams! If you want to lose weight, to move somewhere new, or to learn a new language—whatever it is, there is hope for you, and you need to be spreading this message. With the lack of hope in our world today, we need all hands on deck spreading this message.

There are many messages to spread with texts, social media pages, blogs, and websites, but hope has to be an important part of those messages.

We have said it before, and you'll see it throughout the book—this isn't about money. This is about spreading hope and helping people solve their biggest struggles.

PART TWO

WHAT TO USE
THAT WORKS

CHAPTER 4

TOO MANY PEOPLE ARE TRYING TO CHASE INFLUENCERS WITH YOU

The *Starve the Doubts* podcast is beginning to see moderate success a year and half after its debut. Jared remembers buying into the pre-podcast launch idea that he needed A-list influencers on the podcast in order to grow an audience and build an online platform. It seemed like a reasonable plan. He could invite special guests on the show, and they would help him promote the episodes because they are nice people, and bingo…some of their fans would add Jared to their guru lists, which would generate an instant podcast audience almost overnight. Right?

Unfortunately, that is not what happened. Jared was fortunate to book some amazing guests on *Starve the Doubts*. He interviewed some incredible folks prior to launching the podcast. His show was introduced to iTunes and Stitcher radio. It was time to re-create success similar to that seen by good people like John Lee Dumas and his top-ranked *Entrepreneur on Fire* podcast.

The analytics for downloads and subscribed listeners did not lie or candy coat the truth about *Starve the Doubts*. No one was listening to Jared's podcast, and almost no one cared in the beginning. It was a difficult pill to swallow. He learned a few hard lessons.

A majority of the influencers and A-listers on his guest wishlist did not have time or interest in being on his new show, which had zero listeners. The guests who were gracious enough to give him the time for an interview were not inclined to share it with their audiences. Finally, the guests who did give him their time, and who also shared the show with their networks on social media, did not translate into a large *Starve the Doubts* audience that listened to the guest interviews and subscribed or stuck around as well.

Jared is grateful that he went through that experience. It almost caused him to quit, but he was fortunate to learn some valuable lessons that are shared in this book. If you're trying to connect with an influencer just to promote your business, they'll see right through it. Influencers are smart entrepreneurs and can smell fake motives a mile away.

Besides yourself, there are thousands of other people trying to connect with them. In an interview, *New York Times* best-selling author Chris Guillebeau revealed that he gets 200 to 300 e-mails every day. Chances are that a good amount of those e-mails are from people trying to connect with him.

Your attempts to connect with an influencer will get lost in the crowd, and chances are it won't even be seen because influencers often have protocols in place to keep the multitudes at bay. Persistence won't help you; you'll just come off as a stalker.

Can we be honest for a minute about what actually works today and what matters? Kimanzi would like to share a little story.

In 2012, Kimanzi started to figure out all this online-business stuff and make real money. His two self-published books had sold over 40,000 copies by mid-2012, at a profit of $3.78 a book. He wishes he could have saved that money, but every dollar was used to pay off debt.

After his debts were paid, he was back to square one, and had to figure out how to generate income outside the self-published books. He hit the Internet hard again, trying to figure out the missing piece of the puzzle.

The Internet can be a blessing and a curse because there's plenty of information, but it's hard to know what is relevant. When Kimanzi researched, he saw a ton of different things he could do to make money and the numbers he should focus on.

He was told to focus on his social media following, because that's where people are. He was told to focus on his analytics, because they tell you what people want. He was told to focus on a lot of numbers, but at the end of the day there were only two numbers that really mattered and helped him build a business that now supports his family of five.

THE REACH OF SOCIAL MEDIA

Facebook is now a publicly traded company and because of that it has to generate income where it can. Facebook's representatives made the announcement that your organic reach is decreasing even more, and if you want to reach more people, you're going to have to pay.

The average life of a tweet is ten seconds. Yes, you can schedule multiple tweets throughout the day using something like the Buffer app. A Twitter stream goes fast, and if someone is following a lot of people, your tweet will likely get lost in the mix.

The truth is that people don't buy directly from social media, especially when you're not well known or if you have a smaller following. The truth is that you don't need a huge social media following if you want to reach people on social media. You just have to pay for it or engage people enough to share your content.

Kimanzi has 1,500 likes on his Facebook fan page, but running Facebook ads and encouraging shares has helped him reach over 100,000 people this year. Think about that: he doesn't have that many likes, but that many people have seen his content.

Engagement and ads have helped Kimanzi generate $10,000 in income. Even though he's seen these numbers, people didn't buy from that page. All social media did was lead people back to his website, and that's where the sales happened.

Could you argue that he needed social media to generate that income? Sure, but social media shouldn't have been his focus as he was building. These results came *after* he already had something established. His number one goal is to help you figure out where to spend the limited time you have as you build.

Increasingly, social media platforms will head to a pay-for-reach model, which means your organic reach will be less and less. If that's where your entire focus is, you'll be scratching your head later figuring out what to do.

Remember all the people who focused on Google AdWords and lost it all when Google changed its algorithm? You don't want to be in that boat, especially where your income is considered.

THE NUMBERS THAT HELPED BRING IN REAL MONEY

At the end of the day and after three years of building, these are the two numbers that mattered the most as we built our online businesses.

1. E-mail subscribers

These days it's irritating to get a lot of e-mail, so when someone can look past that and sign up for your e-mail list, they're really interested in what you have to say. They're giving you permission to speak to them about what you have going on.

No matter what friends or followers you lose on social media, or how much reach you have, you can still communicate with your e-mail list and send your content. When you start selling something, the people on your e-mail list are the ones most likely to buy it.

Think about it logically: Is one of your close Facebook friends who quickly sees your new course or book likely to click on the link you share and buy? Or is that person who's been reading your blog for a year and loves your free content more likely to make a purchase?

The people on your e-mail list will outsell any other platform two to one. You can send your e-mail subscribers deals and exclusive offers, and they will most likely be repeat customers. We can vouch for this from personal experience.

The coaching clients we have right now all started as people who read our blogs, bought our books, took the free coaching consultation call, and then ended up buying the highest thing we sell on our websites.

When you're building, if your goal is to build something online that supports you, focus the limited amount of time and resources you have on building and nurturing your e-mail list.

If you have twenty people on your e-mail list, you should know all twenty of those people by name. You should be there and help them on a one-on-one basis. When you give them that level of attention, they will tell the whole world about you because no one else online approaches building that way. That's how you will stand out from the 250 million other blogs out there.

2. Income

Look, you're trying to build something that supports your family, and you're trying to replace your current income with this thing. How will it ever do that if you don't focus on generating income?

We're not telling you that money should be your sole focus, because it shouldn't, but too often we lean too far in the other direction and don't think about money at all. When we tell you to focus on income, we mean you should focus how well you can convert with what you already have and what you can create that will help your target audience.

Instead of spending time building social media, which might help you at some point, focus on how to generate income now.

THE RIGHT FOCUS MAKES THIS THING SUPPORT YOU

Look, it all works hand in hand. Yes, you need to build your social media presence. Yes, you should do all the other things it takes to build your online business. However, when you're starting out or when you don't have a huge online presence, you need to have the right focus—especially when you have a limited amount of time.

When you focus on the e-mail list, which leads to the income, real money starts coming in. There's a ton of advice out there from influencers, but most of it is only relevant if you have a large following. Our goal is always to help those who are building and give you what has worked for us.

Right now, Kimanzi has 1,500 Facebook likes, 2,700 Twitter followers, 485 LinkedIn connections, 377 followers on Google+, and 19,000 e-mail subscribers. Compared to the A-listers, these numbers are really small.

Jared has 2,375 Facebook friends, 4,270 Twitter followers, more than 500 LinkedIn connections, 1,944 Google+ followers, and 373 e-mail subscribers.

With an online presence this size, we have online businesses that generate *$15,000 a month* consistently. Look at the numbers again. Look where Kimanzi's and Jared's focus is, and look at what that focus does for their families' bottom line. Social media is great, but nothing beats the e-mail list!

PRACTICAL APPLICATION

We want to give you something practical that you can use. For the next week, look at the amount of time you use to build your dream on the side. When you think about that time, plan on using 60 percent of it on things that build and nurture your e-mail list.

The rest of that time can be spent on everything else. Log the results and play around with the percentages. See what it does for your bottom line. We think the results will surprise you!

While most people are focused on connecting with influencers, you should focus on what matters. Focus on building your business, and spend your time on connecting with those you serve.

We talk a lot about e-mail lists. Your e-mail list is important, so you should understand the types of e-mails that no one opens.

Smart entrepreneurs are always looking for new business. One tried-and-true method we use is e-mail marketing. Entrepreneurs are always looking for new tactics that get potential new customers to open their e-mails.

Learning and testing are the keys to figuring out what works, but there are three e-mails that won't turn that lead into a customer. The reason e-mail marketing has gotten such a bad rap is because of e-mail spam.

You may have used these e-mails because you were taught they work or just because e-mail marketing isn't your strong suit. Either way, if you want to build your business through e-mail, *avoid* the following types of e-mails.

The "Quick Question" E-mail

In this type of e-mail your goal is to convince the recipient that you have some quick information that will blow his or her mind. The subject line is designed to be "click bait." Many people suggest using this type of e-mail to connect with influencers.

The "quick question" e-mail usually looks something like this:

> I just want to ask you a quick question. How would you like to make more money than you thought possible?

You may not say "money," but insert some cheesy line that people see right through. The problem is that once the recipient realizes what's going on, he or she will delete the e-mail and never do business with you. Influencers will flag your e-mail as spam. Be direct. People don't have time to entertain e-mail games.

If you're really sincere about asking a quick question or offering some quick advice, contact the person on Twitter. One hundred and forty characters will test your motives.

The "This Is What You're Missing" E-mail

This type of e-mail points out where the recipient is lacking. These e-mails usually look something like the following:

> I noticed you only have 500 Facebook fans. You need to have at least 2,000 for people to respect your company.

> I noticed you're not ranking on the first page of Google. Our company can get you on the front page and bring you thousands of new visitors.

These types of e-mails sound helpful, but they're actually very irritating to the person who receives them. You may have the best pitch in the world, but the recipients will never do business with you because this makes the wrong first impression.

Peter Drucker has said that people buy with their hearts, not their minds. When you upset new leads right off the bat, they'll be thinking about how they'll never do business with you.

Your goal with the first e-mail to a potential new customer should be to establish a relationship. People buy from someone they know, like, and trust. Those initial e-mails should be packed with value and amazing content that shows potential new customers that you know what you're talking about. When they get value from that first e-mail, they will open your next e-mails.

This is how you establish trust and authority in your industry. This is how you separate yourself from your competition. Many entrepreneurs will try to overwhelm leads with fancy marketing schemes. In the long run that's not what grows your business.

The "I Made Seven Figures Using this System" E-mail

This type of e-mail goes over the top showing potential new customers the amazing results your product or service delivers.

Once they see the results, they'll be hitting that buy button before they have even finished reading the e-mail.

These e-mails don't work because recipients probably won't believe you. There have been some Internet marketers who make it hard to believe anyone's claims.

People buy from someone they trust. If your first e-mail is a claim that they don't believe, you have lost that trust and any chance to gain it back.

It's a stretch to think that you can send a cold e-mail to someone who doesn't know you or your company and get him or her to buy from you. It happens, but it's the exception, not the rule.

There are better ways to handle your e-mail marketing efforts. These methods won't deliver instant results, but over time they will increase your bottom line.

Focus on building a relationship with new leads. Focus on better headlines that gets your e-mails opened and deliver value that help recipients solve their biggest problems.

There is no easy road when it comes to e-mail marketing. It can be highly profitable for your business if you avoid cliché e-mails.

We bet you're now wondering what types of e-mails people *do* open. What's the best way to do e-mail marketing?

With the rise of social media has come a decline in e-mail marketing for some entrepreneurs. This is a mistake, because e-mail marketing is still a highly effective way to increase sales for your business.

In 2013, 3.6 billion people had e-mail accounts, according to Jeff Bullas. It's estimated that by 2016 that number will increase to 4.3 billion people. Social media is a great way to generate leads, but through e-mail you can convert those leads into customers.

Smart entrepreneurs use e-mail marketing to create new business and turn customers into repeat customers. E-mail marketing can be one of the best tools in your marketing arsenal if it's done right.

TWEAKING YOUR E-MAIL MARKETING EFFORTS

The frustration with e-mail comes when entrepreneurs use dated techniques or rely too heavily on social media. There are a few tweaks you can make that will greatly help your e-mail marketing efforts.

Offer an incentive to get people to sign up.

Entrepreneurs know the value of offering a free digital download or video as an incentive to get people to sign up for their e-mail list. The problem is that most of these "gifts" are terrible.

Legendary entrepreneur Ramit Sethi says your free content should be better than most people's paid content. With over 500,000 monthly readers, he definitely practices what he preaches. When you can master this philosophy, you create lifelong customers.

It's worth your time to create a free gift that will make signing up for your e-mail list a no-brainer. When someone gets incredible value from your free content, they are more likely to buy your premium content.

Use automation.

One of the great things about e-mail marketing is that you can have automated campaigns running 24/7. With services like MailChimp, AWeber, and Infusionsoft, you can set up autoresponders.

These campaigns are designed to encourage new customers to get to know your company and, eventually, what your company offers. Automating e-mails frees up your time to work on your other marketing efforts.

Focus on the little things.

Many entrepreneurs don't encourage respondents to open their e-mails because they're missing some of the basics:

- Strong headlines

- Researching the best time to send out e-mails

- Keeping e-mails straight to the point

- E-mail presentation

- Clear takeaways for readers

Making tweaks here and there can dramatically increase your open rates. When you have a captive audience, you create an opportunity to close the sale.

Send out exclusive content.

Your e-mail list should feel like a club that only VIPs are allowed to attend. At least once a month, you should send out exclusive content just for your e-mail list.

Your e-mail recipients will realize the value and stay subscribed. If the exclusive content is good, they'll recommend your e-mail list to other people. They will make it a point to open every e-mail you send out.

Don't be afraid to sell.

To build an e-mail list, entrepreneurs create a ton of free content. Whether it's a blog, podcast, or videos, use free content to establish your authority. The problem comes when you only offer free content but don't sell regularly. When you do get around to selling, people opt out like crazy because you've confused them. You've trained them to only expect free content, so they don't want to be sold to.

You also shouldn't be on the other end of the spectrum. You don't want to come off as the sleazy marketer who's always selling. A smart entrepreneur can figure out the right balance.

Continue to grow your list.

Whether you have an e-mail list of fifty people or 500,000, you should always work on growing your list. People will come and go, so adding new names is vital to keeping your list healthy.

We live in an unprecedented time where social media and the Internet have created tremendous opportunities to grow a subscriber list of engaged fans and future customers.

Take full advantage of social media, webinars, video, guest posting, and joint ventures to grow your e-mail list. Grow that list and nurture it.

Over the years e-mail marketing has gained a bad rap because of spam. Realize that spam is everywhere, even on social media. People still respond to the right kind of e-mails.

If you can use these techniques to make your e-mail marketing efforts better, your influence and income will increase. Use social media, but don't neglect e-mail. It's not going anywhere.

Shenee Howard had some challenges starting her business. In 2011, she was broke (her wages were being garnished for student loan debt), confused, living with her parents, and struggling to get clients. She knew she needed a change, but she wasn't sure where to begin.

She decided to try something out of desperation, and it made a powerful impact on her business. Shenee started talking to people—one hundred people, to be exact. She decided to speak with one hundred people individually for fifteen minutes each. She collected the data. It gave her clarity. It helped her to identify her ideal customer. She also identified whom she didn't want to work with.

She was able to get sales copy from the conversations and experience. Four months later Shenee sold out her first product launch, which was designed based on what her target client wanted. In fact, many of the people who signed up for that first class were part of the one hundred people Shenee interviewed. She has not looked back since.

With the 100 People Project, she now helps others who are feeling lost about what they are doing, who they are creating products and services for, and how to make money (http://heyshenee.com/labs/#peeps). Chris Guillebeau even asked Shenee to share her story on stage at the Pioneer Nation Conference in March 2014.

You can listen to Shenee's story here: http://www.starvethedoubts.com/105-shenee-howard-100-people-project/.

Could you spend some time talking with one hundred people for fifteen minutes each in order to get clarity and create products and services that address the problems of your target market? Would that be a better way to spend your time than what you are currently doing?

There is a lot of competition to get an influencer's attention. This chapter was written to show you that you can build your business on your own.

CHAPTER 5

CHANCES ARE YOU WON'T GET THE RESULT YOU'RE LOOKING FOR

Influencers are busy entrepreneurs. Even if you get the chance to connect, their response to you will be very limited and tailored to not open room for another conversation.

If your dream is to get that mention on their podcast or that tweet promoting your business, it probably won't happen. Sure, there are exceptions to every rule, but those aren't the norm.

When you do get a chance to connect with an influencer it will mean more for you than them. They will be polite, of course, but they're not thinking about how you can work together.

EXAMPLE 1: PAID VS. PRO BONO

Jared bought into the idea when he started his podcast that interviewing top entrepreneurs would greatly increase the visibility of the show and kick-start the growth of a massive audience. He wishes he could tell you that everything turned out that way.

Jared was fortunate to interview top experts and influencers in business. Many of his guests were gracious to give him their time. He was excited to have the opportunities to speak with his heroes and share the conversations on the podcast. It turns out he was practically the only one excited about sharing it. He admits he was initially disappointed when almost all of the experts featured on the podcast did not share the interviews with their networks on social media.

Jared began to question himself when this happened. He became discouraged and wondered if his show was any good. What did he do wrong? He made a strategic decision to further pour valuable time and resources into several of the influencers who were guests on his podcast, thinking that would help him grow. Jared believed they could help and were looking out for him.

The following stories are not shared out of bitterness, but as a warning to hopefully prevent you from making similar mistakes. Jared has left out the names of the individuals, but he's happy to chat about this further if you want to tweet him at @jaredeasley using the hashtag #StopChasingInfluencers.

Jared spent thousands of dollars attending multiple events presented by one influencer. He bought plane tickets and paid for hotel rooms as well. Let's call this influential gentleman "Tom." Jared believed that attending Tom's events would help his business and that supporting the events would grant him a stronger connection with Tom. Tom had the answers, so a connection with him was important.

Jared's plan worked in the sense that it gave him a limited audience with Tom. Tip: buying the products and services of an influencer is probably the best way to "connect" with him or her. Jared spoke with Tom in person at his events on several occasions.

He and Tom even talked about the possibility of Jared working with Tom at various future events as a paid member of his team.

Jared will never forget listening to Tom provide a compelling message about pricing your products and services. Tom encouraged the attendees to charge what they were worth. The message really resonated with Jared. It made him believe that he was capable of charging more for his services because of the value provided.

A few months later Jared was approached via e-mail by one of Tom's assistants. She asked if he would act as the road manager for Tom on one of his upcoming speaking trips. He normally had a particular team member handle this, but the team member was unavailable for one reason or another. The opportunity was time sensitive. They needed Jared to respond quickly. He was super excited and eager, to say the least. He knew that getting this time with Tom would be very valuable. They discussed travel forms and filling out a W-9. Tom's assistant asked Jared what he would charge to take on this one-time role (at least one-time for now).

Jared was so grateful that he attended Tom's event. He was adequately equipped and knew not to undercharge for this particular opportunity. After all, Tom is a man of integrity. He would be proud of Jared for implementing his advice.

Jared offered to do the assignment for $300 a day (still grossly undercharging). The trip would take two days, and Tom was likely to make no less than $15,000 for the one-hour keynote session. Jared believed that $300 was not being greedy, and was ready to take the assignment and give Tom his absolute best.

Tom's assistant replied and asked Jared to clarify his price. She wanted to know if he was charging $300 for the entire project or for a day. He replied and told her he needed $300 a day (which he had already mentioned in the previous e-mail, but perhaps had not been clear).

Tom's assistant later replied:

> Jared,
>
> Thanks for getting back to me. At this time, we would like to pass on having you accompany Tom.
>
> Thanks again.

Jared was confused. He started to question whether he had asked for too much money. He responded to Tom's assistant to ask her if they needed to adjust the price in order to move forward with the opportunity. She offered no explanation and simply told Jared that they were no longer interested.

As providence would have it, Jared had a podcast interview the following day with another member of Tom's management team (the timing of this was a coincidence, but also ironic). The interview was fantastic. Jared asked the guest afterward if he could get his opinion on his recent situation with Tom. Tom's team member basically told Jared that he should not have charged *anything* in order to get the opportunity. Really? This is contrary to what Tom teaches at his events.

Jared never realized up to that point that Tom was someone who teaches, "Do as I say and not as I do." He felt like a fool.

He continued building his business and growing his network. Months later Jared received a message from another member of Tom's team. Tom was conveniently inviting Jared to be an affiliate for his upcoming product launch. Jared was thrilled to decline the option.

How many events, products, and services do you think Jared purchased from Tom after this situation? The answer is zero.

What would you have done in this scenario if you had spent thousands of dollars supporting someone and taken their advice when they offered you an opportunity, only to learn that the advice conveniently did not apply to doing business with them?

EXAMPLE 2: YOUR SUCCESS COULD BE PERCEIVED AS A THREAT OR DISTRACTION

Jared remembers the day he was let go from his former day job as a project manager. He was discouraged by the sudden shock of the event. It was December 2013, and Christmas was right around the corner. Jared has a wife, a three-year-old daughter, a mortgage, and various other responsibilities, like most people. He felt like the weight of the world was on his shoulders. He navigated through the holidays and traveled to Las Vegas to speak at New Media Expo. He was thrilled to have his first major speaking opportunity at a large and reputable event. He was concerned about finances, but the moment was in front of him and he was embracing the *carpe diem* mind-set.

Jared felt fortunate to meet a highly successful and influential person at this event. He had interviewed this gentleman on his podcast before and had a small connection with him. Let's give him the name "Jim." Jim learned about Jared's work situation and asked how he was doing. They had an honest conversation about Jared's status. Jim later came back and offered a contracted position to work with him and his team on their upcoming major event. Jared was super grateful for this, and felt as though it was the answer to prayer or his lucky break at the time. Jared's family would be able to count on this income to help them as he continued to grow his business.

Jared connected with Jim's right-hand man, "Paul." Paul and Jared started to work together on planning various projects and aspects related to their major event. Everything seemed to be going well. Jared did not have a lot of work with Paul and Jim, but was happy to jump in when needed or called upon.

Jared was working with his business partners on the initial ideas and concepts for the Podcast Movement (http://podcastmovement.com) at the time. They were preparing for an upcoming—and what would later become epic—Kickstarter campaign (http://starvethedoubts.com/kickstarter). The preparation for the Podcast Movement crowd-funding campaign never crossed wires with the projects that Jared was working on with Paul and Jim.

In fact, Paul was so happy with Jared's work that he was named a Network Ambassador for their event. He had his biography and picture on the speaker page and was thrilled about it. *Progress!* He felt as though a lot of his generous connections and hard work in the past was finally paying off. He was also tasked to lead some round-table discussions about podcasting. It *seemed* as though everything was going well.

The Kickstarter campaign for Podcast Movement launched, raising its minimum amount of $11,000 in eight hours! The event was all over social media. It was a huge success with amazing momentum. Jared believed that they would be successful, but he did not anticipate this happening so quickly. The timing was great, but it was also the same time that Jim and Paul were heavily promoting their event as well.

Jared had a few conversations with Paul a few days after the successful launch of the Podcast Movement Kickstarter campaign. He never mentioned it on the first call. He mentioned on the second call that he needed to talk about the Podcast Movement to make sure that there were no conflicts of interest. Jared agreed and they scheduled a conversation for Friday morning. Everything was fine...until Friday morning.

Paul called Jared to tell him that Paul and Jim were no longer willing to work with him. They fired Jared immediately as a contractor with no explanation.

Fast forward to several months later. Jim had communication with one of the sponsors for Podcast Movement about the possibility of being included as a speaker during their presentation. Jared and his business partners were surprised because of Jared's previous encounter with Jim. They believed that having Jim at their event—at no cost, by the way—would offer a greater perceived value to their attendees. Jared reached out to Jim after months of silence between them to clear the air and get his perspective on speaking at the event. Their e-mail conversation follows. Note that a few names were changed for privacy.

> Good evening, Jim,
>
> Thank you for being willing to speak as a part of the Sponsor's session at Podcast Movement. I was surprised by this decision considering our history, but grateful just the same. I am looking forward to seeing you in Dallas.
>
> Best regards,
>
> Jared Easley

> Hey, Jared,
>
> It's my hope you can put that history behind you. I think you are a good guy and it just didn't work out for us at that time because you had other things on the horizon (like this) and we needed more than you could give then. I am excited to network with fellow podcasters and have purchased my plane ticket

and reserved my hotel room. Hopefully you guys can list me among the speakers. Again, I hold no ill will against you and hope you feel the same.

Jim

Jim came to the event and was featured as a fellow speaker. The hosts were happy to have him there. Jared believes in providence—some people call it karma. He was discouraged and disappointed when he was fired from Jim's company for what seemed to be no reason. However, it was ironic that the greater narrative had Jim speaking at the Podcast Movement, which happened to be the very event Jared was fired for being a part of.

Kimanzi has casually connected with many influencers many times, both in person and through e-mail. He was excited thinking he was forming relationships that someday could help his business. You know how the story goes, I'm sure. Those connections were only in his mind.

After the conference was over or at some point in the e-mail chain, reality set in. They were being polite, but there was no interest in really connecting. It took years to realize that if this was going to happen, Kimanzi was going to make it happen on his own.

If you can connect with an influencer, that's great. We're not saying you should never talk to them. We just want you to be realistic about your expectations. You can do this on your own, and when you do, you can connect with them as equals.

CHAPTER 6

IT'S NOT THE KEY TO YOUR SUCCESS

Getting a shout-out from someone at the top of your industry isn't what makes you successful. What makes you successful is serving your customers and creating solutions to their biggest problems.

When you do this, your business will be talked about. If you want your heroes to notice you, it would be best if someone other than yourself told them about you. Your success can't depend on anyone else; otherwise you won't be in business very long.

Abbie Unger is someone who achieved success without influencers. Abbie is definitely one of those fire-starters. Abbie was a former flight attendant who turned her passion into an incredible business. The business is super specific, which means she doesn't have to have a huge audience. Abbie is in her own world helping people fulfill their dreams of becoming flight attendants. She has helped over forty people land jobs as flight attendants.

She's got a full schedule of coaching clients, she's selling her book and products, and she has a Facebook group that includes over 10,000 people! On top of all that, Facebook featured her story. Let us repeat: Facebook itself featured her story! Way to go, Abbie!

Abbie is living proof that influencers aren't the key to success. Serve your audience and deliver incredible value. Helping those you serve is what makes you successful.

Building a business that supports your family is what makes you successful. Your success doesn't come from a pat on the back. Your success comes when you experience true freedom in your life. Success comes from putting yourself in the right places.

What does it take to be successful? Sometimes it's putting yourself in the right places and being around the right people. You've probably heard Jim Rohn say you're the average of the five people you hang out with. It's true, and if you're in situations or around certain people, you won't make any progress.

The only way we finally made traction was putting ourselves in the right situations and being surrounded by the right people.

CONFERENCES

Amazing conferences happen every day—conferences that can teach you what you need to know. You can use these opportunities to network with people who can help your success.

For a long time we were afraid to invest in ourselves. After attending some conferences, we saw the value and invested in two really amazing experiences. We also started speaking and got to attend sessions at these conferences.

We wish we had applied all that we learned at those conferences. We wish we had stayed in touch with the amazing people we met. Learn from our mistakes.

If you have a chance to attend a conference that can help you and your business, do it. Don't drain your bank account to attend, but if you have a little extra cash, look for conferences that will help.

COACHING

You may know that we coach, so we're a little biased. If we're honest with you, we prefer coaching to conferences. You can go to an amazing conference and learn a ton. You then come home and start implementing, but will end up with questions on how to proceed. If the conference is over, how do you get your questions answered? Most of the time you're figuring it out on your own.

What we really like about coaching is that you have someone to answer all your questions immediately. The key lies in picking the right coach. If you find the right coach, you can get personal help that's specific to your situation.

There are too many coaches who talk the talk but can't back up what they're saying. Look for a coach who gets results. What kind of testimonials do they have from previous customers?

Conferences tend to teach general principles that may not be best for where you are. Again, let us stress that it depends on the coach and conference.

MASTERMINDS

There's nothing like bouncing your ideas by a group of people who will be honest and help you out. There's nothing like contributing and learning from people who are taking action.

If you're not in a group, you should join a good one or start your own. The advice we would give you is to look for people who are where you're at or slightly ahead. You don't want to be in a group where you're pretty much giving them a group coaching session.

GOOD SOCIAL MEDIA GROUPS

Just like a good mastermind group, you can join amazing social media groups. There are groups for book launches, careers, business, and so on. You name it, and there's probably a group for it.

You can also create great groups. Our friend Abbie has a group for flight attendants, which has 10,000 members and is still growing. She tells us stories that bring a smile to her face.

Look for those good groups or create one of your own. The right group will give you tremendous value. Put yourself around the right people and right situations and you will create success. Learn, contribute, and grow, and don't be afraid to invest in yourself.

If you're hanging out with negative people, they will drag you and your dream down. Surround yourself with people who will be honest but will also help you in any way they can.

You are your own key to success, not a shout-out from someone on the top. Choose yourself and believe in your success. Success starts with the right mind-set. Success means living a happy life.

THE RIGHT MIND-SET

In July 2011, Kimanzi hit the lowest point of his life. He was 170 pounds overweight, he was at a job he absolutely hated, and he lived in a place that made him worried about his family's safety. Oh, yeah, and he owed over $180,000 to the IRS (almost forgot about that one).

One day that July, Kimanzi was sitting on the couch crying as everything came crashing down on his head at the same time. The straw that broke the camel's back was separating from his wife. Every day they fought about everything because of all the problems Kimanzi had brought into their lives.

Kimanzi sat there that day with the TV on, not really thinking about what he was watching. A commercial came on showing this happy family playing on the beach. They were laughing. He wondered why that couldn't be his family.

Today Kimanzi's life is a miracle. He is truly happy, and it happened in ways that he would have never expected. He searched and searched for the answers to happiness. They were right under his nose.

If you're struggling or if you just want to live a happier life, Kimanzi has these tips that can help you get there.

Sleep more.

At the end of the day a lot of the reason we feel the way we do can be contributed to not getting enough sleep. When you don't have enough energy for the day, it naturally affects how you feel and your attitude.

Sleep is something we know we need; yet we don't get enough it of consistently. How much sleep should you get? That's specific to each of us, but we can tell you that you can always use more.

If you look at some of the successful people in our history, you'll see they average around seven hours of sleep a night. Doctors have a lot to say about not getting enough sleep and all the health problems it leads to.

When Kimanzi was depressed during the rough times, he compounded the problem with lack of sleep. He slept three to four hours a night, which wasn't healthy. He was a jerk, and he gained weight from the odd hours and lack of motivation.

If you're feeling drained or a little down, try getting an extra hour of sleep every night. Turn off the prime-time TV shows and go to bed a little earlier. You'll wake up refreshed and ready to tackle your day.

Exercise.

Once you've tackled any sleep issues, it's time to move more. At his heaviest Kimanzi was 370 pounds. He woke up and looked at his reflection in the mirror and hated life. His happiness could definitely be linked to his weight.

He started slowly by walking for thirty minutes a day. After he started to lose a few pounds and feel better, he started running. Over the course of a year, between exercise and eating right, he was able to lose 160 pounds.

Running may not be your thing, but find some sort of physical activity that you can do that will get your heart pumping. Start slow, and if at all possible, start your day with exercise. When you do you'll have the energy you need all day. It's an amazing and mind-refreshing way to start your day.

The stats are staggering as to what exercise can do for your body and state of mind. They're also staggering to the crisis we face with our health.

With the weight gone, Kimanzi has more confidence and more energy. He's more productive, and all of this has led to living a happier life. His wife is also happy having half a husband. If exercise isn't part of your life, you should add it. You'll see amazing results, and it will lead to a happier life.

Do work you love.

Yeah, we know, easier said than done. Right? There are many physical and mental issues that can arise from doing work you hate.

Kimanzi can tell you that the job he hated was part of the reason for his weight gain, lack of sleeping, and lack of happiness. Even when he wasn't at work, he still thought about it, and it affected his attitude in a negative way.

Finding or creating a job you love is hard. It's also not one of those things you can change overnight. However, if you start working on it today, you can get closer to finding or creating work you love.

If you listen to the news, you'll hear how bad our economy is and how there are no opportunities. As you're reading this, realize that today, 2.5 billion people will also be online with you.

If you've ever wanted to start a business or help a current business, there's never been a better place than the Internet. Every day people are experiencing true freedom by having online businesses. You can also use the Internet to find that job you love.

Kimanzi started on the journey to creating an online business in 2011. Now, in 2014, he's writing this chapter from his home in Maui, Hawaii, completely supported by his online business. It's not easy, but it is possible.

The point is that you spend forty to sixty hours of your week working. One way or another it will affect you. If you're not happy with your work, start the process today. Take the first step, even if it's a baby step.

Stop comparing.

It's natural to compare where you are or what's happening in your life to what someone else is going through. If someone experiences success, we tend to want to compare ourselves with him or her. Don't do it!

As Kimanzi made big changes in his life, one way he measured his progress was by comparing his results to what others were doing. He learned the hard way that comparing yourself to others only leads to bitterness and heartache.

Your journey is *your* journey, and it shouldn't be compared. Make changes at your pace. As long as you're moving forward, you'll get there. If someone gets there before you, congratulate him or her and then focus on your journey.

Getting caught up in the comparison game won't help you. If you want to live a happy life, live *your* life. Once Kimanzi stopped comparing and really focused, change happened.

You can live a happier life if you decide you want to, and take action to back up that decision.

Kimanzi lost 170 pounds and left that job he hated to write, speak, and coach full time. He moved from Milwaukee, Wisconsin, to Maui, Hawaii. He wakes up every day happy and excited for what the future holds. It took three years of hard struggle, but he can tell you after the storm there's always a rainbow.

You have the power. Life is too short to live and then die with regret. Do something about it. Start today. Work on these four areas and we guarantee you'll be living a happier life.

Which one of these are you working on? Which one do you need to work on?

PART THREE

A BETTER STRATEGY

CHAPTER 7

YOU CAN BECOME
AN INFLUENCER

If you're going to do this, you have to understand something. Impact is more important than income.

When entrepreneurs start a business, one major goal is to generate income. Without income the business will quickly fail. In our efforts to generate income, however, too many of us miss the most important part of building a business.

The word *impact* is defined as "influence; effect." When an entrepreneur makes an impact, her or his influence continues far beyond this lifetime. A great example of this is Steve Jobs and Apple. Steve is gone, but his influence lives on through the amazing company he created that impacts millions of lives every day.

While we want to generate income for our businesses, creating an impact is what takes your business to the next level. Here's why you should focus more on impact than income (http://www.entrepreneur.com/article/234271).

IMPACT CREATES PASSIVE INCOME

In 1989, Stephen R. Covey published a popular book titled *The 7 Habits of Highly Effective People.* This book has sold over 25 million copies, has been translated into forty languages, and consistently appears on *The New York Times* best-seller list twenty-five years later. Covey passed away in 2012, but his impact continues on, and so does the passive income from book sales.

When you release a book, movie, music, or some kind of product, the passive income will continue if that product has made an impact on people's lives. Covey's book has made such a huge impact that we don't doubt it will still sell twenty-five years from now. And every year the passive income will continue to flow.

Your business has the opportunity to do the same thing, even if it's not a book. When you create something that helps people and makes an impact on their lives, that impact will keep the sales continually flowing.

IMPACT BUILDS YOUR BRAND AND BUSINESS

Apple, Zappos, Microsoft, and many other familiar companies started as little more than a name and an idea. What made them into the powerhouses they are today is the impact they made on people's lives, through their vision and what they created.

In the world of entrepreneurship today, there are millions of businesses, many of them selling similar products. The best way for your business to stand out is to focus on the impact you can make, not by being a clone.

When you speak to your target audience's biggest struggles and solve them, they will tell everyone they know and spread your impact. Word of mouth is the strongest form of marketing because people are exposed to you and your business through people they trust. This is the best way to build a brand. How many people told you to read Stephen R. Covey's book? That's why the book remains a best seller after twenty-five years (http://www.entrepreneur.com/article/222971).

IMPACT CHANGES LIVES

There have been many one-hit wonders in the world of entrepreneurship. Remember NEXT? The company Steve Jobs created after he was fired from Apple? Next is gone, but Apple grows.

It's estimated that 600,000 to 1 million books are published each year. Many of these books won't sell more than 250 copies. Yet a book published twenty-five years ago continues to sell millions of copies. The difference is the impact certain books have on changing people's lives. Too many books are written just to make money. Too many products and services are created with the main goal of creating income. They usually don't stand the test of time.

When your business has a hand in changing someone's life, that person becomes a walking testimonial and constant marketing campaign. The world of entrepreneurship is flooded with hype, so when someone sees the real thing, she or he won't hesitate to buy.

Owning a business is great for so many reasons. It provides freedom and a chance to build something that you can pass on to your children. It can be even greater than that if you shift the focus away from simply making money. Your business can become just as worthwhile as any of the companies that have stood the test of time.

When you create products and services that make a real difference in people's lives, you separate yourself from everyone else.

When you make an impact on people's lives in a positive way, you create lifelong customers who become your company's evangelists.

We live in a pretty amazing time. No longer can the old-school gatekeepers keep us from doing the things we want to do in our businesses. Look what self-publishing has done for authors.

There are many ways to become an influencer, including the following:

- Build a huge social media following.

- Write for an authority website like *Entrepreneur,* among many others.

- Interview on radio shows, TV shows, and podcasts.

- Serve an industry so well that you become the go-to person in it.

There are many paths you can take, and these are going to be a good use of your time. Chasing influencers may have worked in the past, but, honestly, it's a played-out strategy.

Smart entrepreneurs always focus on innovating. They strive to be square pegs in the round holes, as Steve Jobs said. There aren't many new ideas these days, but what makes you stand out from everyone else doing the same thing is being unique to yourself. Let chasing influencers be someone else's strategy. Build your business differently.

In this next section, we lay out the specific-strategy stuff that helps you become your own influencer without that shout-out from someone at the top. We're going to make this very practical so you can start implementing right away.

Remember the end of the last chapter? It all starts with the right mind-set. This means not comparing yourself to other people on your journey. The comparison game is a dream killer.

Have you ever read a social media status update by a friend or acquaintance talking about something great they did or that happened to them? You're happy for them and what they accomplished, but there's something gnawing deep inside you.

Maybe you think, "Why couldn't that be me?" Why aren't you the one who landed that guest post? Why aren't you the one who was accepted to speak at that conference? Why don't you have a "freedom date"?

We've accomplished a lot in this past year. Kimanzi lost 170 pounds and moved from Wisconsin to Maui. He's fully supported by his writing, speaking, and coaching.

Jared released a number-one, best-selling book. He hosted the world's first podcasting conference, Podcast Movement. He has a killer podcast and a great network of friends and peers. Even still, we see these updates and we get jealous.

Our pride reads a guest post on a blog we want to guest post on and says, "I write better than that person." We get that rejection e-mail from a conference a friend was chosen for and we feel jealous.

HANDLING JEALOUSY

Jealousy is a part of human nature, and we're guessing you've been there, too. We want to be happy when people do amazing things, but we want it to be us. We might even want that attention.

There's a line you don't want to cross, and there are ways to deal with jealousy when it arises. Jealousy can eat away at you and keep you from making progress with your dream. Here's how you deal with jealousy.

Step away from the situation.

In that moment when jealousy hits, walk away. Turn your phone, computer, and tablet off, and breathe. If you sit and think, and keep reading or thinking, you're going to let the jealousy build up and become a monster.

Turn on some music or talk to your spouse, but step away and express what you're feeling. Don't hold it inside and let it fester. Get real with your feelings. If you're jealous, that's natural, so don't be ashamed to admit it to yourself or someone else.

Verbalizing those feelings and acknowledging them will help you heal. Really analyze why you're jealous. Maybe it's because there's something you know you need to work on.

Take the focus off yourself

Jealousy may be there, but if it's strong, it's because you're too focused on yourself. You're probably reading this because you're involved in this whole online world. It's easy to get jealous online.

You see some A-lister doing amazing things and you get frustrated and jealous because your online business isn't taking off. Realize why they're doing what they do, and most of the time it's to help people (although there are some bad apples).

Don't focus on their success or compare what they're doing to what you're doing. Instead, focus on those you're serving and how you're helping them. Focus on helping them get through those difficult situations.

This shouldn't be about you. If this is about your pride or ego, you're destined to fail. The ones who succeed online are those who come from a place of service. It's hard, but when you focus on others, you'll get to where those A-listers are.

Be grateful for what you have.

We did a webinar with our friend Jimmy and something he said opened our eyes. He talked about his wife's new car. It was a car he had never heard of. As soon as his wife started driving it, he looked around and started seeing this car everywhere.

It's not that those cars were never there. Once his wife got one, his eyes were opened to what is around him. That's how it is with gratitude in our lives. We don't see all the things around us we should be grateful for until our eyes are opened. Jimmy said he wakes up every day and before his foot hits the ground, he thinks of three things he's grateful for.

We started doing that after hearing him talk. Every morning we think about three specific things we're grateful for. Doing this has opened our eyes to all the amazing things in our lives we have to be grateful for.

If you listed just one thing a day, your eyes would be opened and your attitude would change from jealous to grateful. Instead of being jealous your friend got that guest post, you would be grateful you have a friend who writes that well.

You would be grateful for the day and age we live in, where we can make a living online. We live in a time when social media and things like self-publishing open avenues that weren't open before.

In the end this online stuff isn't about you or the money. It's about helping people get through rough times. It's about making an impact on the world. Don't get jealous or let jealousy win.

This week when you see one of those updates, step away, say one thing you're grateful for, and come back and smile. You're truly blessed! Getting out of the comparison game is how you have the right mind-set.

CONQUER SELF-LIMITING BELIEFS

If you're going to become a success, stop listening to self-limiting beliefs. Every successful entrepreneur had to conquer self-limiting beliefs before she or he could grow his or her business. These beliefs may be buried deep in your mind, or maybe you've verbalized them, but they will keep your business from realizing its full potential.

There will always be areas of your business where you can learn and improve. A wise entrepreneur said that an expert is a student first. However, there's a difference between always striving for improvement and being stuck with self-limiting beliefs (http://www.entrepreneur.com/article/234115).

The key to success in business is constant growth. Your mind-set determines what actions you take to grow your business, which determines the numbers on your bottom line. To have the right mind-set, conquer these self-limiting beliefs.

My content isn't good enough.

Many entrepreneurs question the quality of the material they produce, but the important opinion belongs to your audience. The feedback you receive from your target audience tells you the quality of your content. Here are some ways to know if your content is hitting the mark:

- the open rate of the e-mails you send out

- the engagement with your social media posts

- the comments on your website

- how much people are sharing your content

- constant growth in visitors to your website

- constant growth on your e-mail list

If you're seeing success in these areas, stop second-guessing yourself. When these numbers are where you want them to be, that's OK. There's always room for improvement, but don't let that become a self-limiting belief.

I can't raise my prices.

Money is always an uncomfortable topic, especially when you're asking people to pay you. That uneasiness leads too many entrepreneurs to undercharge for their products and services. You shouldn't be afraid to charge a fair price if you're offering people a solution to their biggest struggles. Successful entrepreneurs charge based on value, not what they think someone is willing to pay. If what you create has value, people will always find a way to pay for it (http://www.entrepreneur.com/article/234115).

There's too much competition.

There are more than 900 million websites and 250 million blogs online, with 175,000 being added every day. There are a lot of entrepreneurs teaching the same things. Despite those numbers, your business can thrive. Many businesses don't grow because they try to blend in. They try to connect with influencers and even try to copy those who are successful. You can't blend in and stand out at the same time. Be different. Embrace what makes you who you are and infuse that into your business. Be the square peg in the round hole.

I don't have enough credentials.

There are places where credentials are a must: doctor, lawyer, chemist, and so on. However, the only credential today's entrepreneur needs is the knowledge that comes through experience.

You can learn things in books and classrooms, but experiencing them in the real world is how you grow as an entrepreneur. Ignore the haters who try to point out your lack of credentials, and focus on those you're helping.

I don't have enough resources.

Starting and growing a business usually requires some sort of financial investment. This holds too many entrepreneurs back from starting or growing their businesses. There are many free resources that can help you start and grow. WordPress alone lets you set up a free website, which is one of the most important parts of your business. If your funds aren't where you want them to be, don't let that become a self-limiting belief.

Today you can use a number of ways to grow your business:

- crowdfunding
- venture capital
- bartering
- building as funds come in

We are entrepreneurs because we don't think nine-to-five. We see problems as opportunities to grow. Not having enough funds is a challenge to think outside of the box. Conquer self-limiting beliefs by getting honest with yourself. Acknowledge them and take the steps to beat them. Focus on creating quality products and services. Focus on those whom your business benefits.

Realize that we live in a time when anything is possible. You have everything you need to take your business to levels you never thought were possible. It starts with your mind-set.

CHAPTER 8

WRITING FOR LARGE WEBSITES

Guest posting is a killer strategy for building your online presence. You write an article for a website that is larger than yours, and they give you three links back to your website.

This is great for gaining exposure to new, larger audiences. It's also killer for the back links it provides to your website. Back links are what ultimately helps with search engine optimization.

This is how Kimanzi built his audience in 2012 when he had ten people a day visiting his website. He saw the value in guest posting and immediately wrote an article for the *Huffington Post*.

One of the editors probably looked at it and laughed. What's wild is that three years later Kimanzi landed an article on the *Huffington Post*, and he's actually a contributing writer for it! He also writes for The Good Men Project (http://goodmenproject.com/author/kimanzi-constable/), *Entrepreneur* magazine (http://www.entrepreneur.com/author/kimanzi-constable), and MindBodyGreen (http://mindbodygreen.com/wc/kimanzi-constable).

One guest post for Michael Hyatt put Kimanzi on the map, and guest posting is still the number one way Kimanzi continues to build traffic and e-mail subscribers. We probably don't need to convince you of the merits of guest posting, so let's move on.

You know it works and you want to do it, but how do you land guest posts on large websites?

Kimanzi has been talking about expanding your horizons. He has talked about guest posting for websites that are outside of your normal circle. You may have thought about those sites and are ready. In this section we give you some tips to land those bigger guest posts and articles on really large websites.

RESEARCH BEFORE YOU WRITE

Since writing for some amazing places, Kimanzi gets a lot of e-mails asking how to write for publications like the *Huffington Post*. The first question he asks is, "What 'vertical' would you write for?"

This normally brings on a lot more questions. We would explain how the verticals work, but you're going to have to do your own research if you want to write for the *Huffington Post*. Think of this as your homework.

The point is that if you're going to write for a large website, you have to understand how things work. What kind of people are reading the website, and what style is the website written in?

Most of the time we write posts and then think of where they should go. That's wrong. You should research *who* you want to write for and *then* write the post.

That post should be targeted for that audience and written in the style of that website. If you were going to write for the *Huffington Post*, what vertical would it fit in? (We just gave you a hint.)

When we say research, we mean thorough research. This doesn't mean skimming over the site and then throwing something together. You should know if the publication even takes guest posts or contributors, and to whom to send your articles.

Kimanzi could have told you exactly who to send your article to at the *Huffington Post* before he ever wrote for it. He had done a ton of research, and that information is available online.

Doing your research is great for writing the right content that gets accepted, and it will also come in handy with figuring out how to get featured. We'll get into that later.

DIG DEEPER

If you follow Kimanzi on social media or listened to his episode of *Starve the Doubts*, you know a secret about him—he's a *huge* Taylor Swift fan. He always gets asked why. The answer is simple: he likes the way she writes music (http://www.starvethedoubts .com/104-kimanzi-constable-are-you-living-or-existing/).

He can completely understand what she's writing, and it speaks to how Kimanzi grew up. Her music goes beyond the normal surface fluff you see in music. That surface level fluff is exactly how Kimanzi used to write.

He was worried about offending people; he was worried it wasn't good writing. He let a lot of things hold him back from opening up and really writing. Once he could let go and really find his voice, he could write deeper content.

Larger websites aren't looking for the fluff. There's too much of that available online, and they want to steer clear of it. They want the deeper content—the kind of content that talks about things other people aren't willing to talk about, content that flies in the face of what is normally written.

Kimanzi wrote an article recently called "5 Reasons Why Social-Media Marketing Is Overrated" for *Entrepreneur* magazine (http://www.entrepreneur.com/article/236584). All the social media experts trashed Kimanzi left and right, but they shared the article like crazy. *Entrepreneur* loved it. The post is original and challenges what we're normally told. That's the kind of content large websites like. Look at the shares and comments.

Kimanzi contributes to a website called The Good Men Project. It gets 2 million weekly visitors, and its tagline is "the conversation no one else is having." Do you think it would take an article on "How to Be a Better Man"? That post is generic and fluff. The Good Men Project wants content that's far deeper than that.

A better post would be "7 Reasons You're Not a Better Man." In that post you would go deep and talk about the things that hold men back, and when we say "things," we mean the things we don't talk about: porn, mental and physical abuse, lying, and cheating.

Digging deeper also means doing research. What you're writing about should be backed up by facts and figures. You should link to incredible content that backs up what you're saying. Kimanzi made some bold statements in his article, but he backed every one of them with research.

You're a writer, so stop holding back and write. Create something that's a little bit outside of your comfort zone and submit it to the The Good Men Project (20 percent of its writers are women) or another large website.

Our goal is to open your mind to see the possibilities. Once you do, we want to teach you how to capitalize on those opportunities. You can write for anyone! Right now we want you to think about three large websites you can write for.

How much research should you do for your guest posts? Are you creating deep content?

We're here because guest posting is one of the best ways to build your audience.

Two articles on the *Huffington Post* (http://www .huffingtonpost.com/kimanzi-constable/6-lessons-moving-to -hawaii_b_5666615.html) and The Good Men Project (http:// goodmenproject.com/featured-content/7-choices-youll-regret-at -the-end-of-your-life-dg/) have directly contributed to 12,000 new e-mail subscribers for Kimanzi in the past two months.

Getting interviewed on podcasts and radio shows is great, but think about where people are listening to those shows. They're in the car, on the way to work, or working out.

If they like what you're saying, they have to remember to look you up later. When they're reading a guest post or article on a large website, and they like it, all they have to do is click a link and they're on your website in seconds. It's instant, and within minutes they can be signing up for your e-mail list. That's the power of a good guest post.

You have to do your research and write deeper content. Let's continue with our tips for getting your guest posts published.

HAVE THE RIGHT PITCH

Having the right pitch means a few things. Let's start with whom to pitch to. Remember when we talked about research? Getting articles featured on large websites only happens when you pitch to the right person.

We talked about the *Huffington Post* and verticals. Have you figured those out yet? Verticals are the categories on the *Huffington Post*. The one Kimanzi normally posts to is Healthy Living.

When you become a contributor at the *Huffington Post*, you can post in whatever vertical you want. If you've done your research, you should know that every vertical has its own editor. For you to have a chance to write for the *Huffington Post*, you have to send your post to the editor of whatever vertical your post fits under.

The *Huffington Post* does have a standard place to submit articles, but can you imagine how many people submit articles every day? One editor told us it was close to 30,000 submissions a day.

To cut through all that, send your article to the right editor. That way you can get a quick yes or no. They're usually very busy, so you should get your answer pretty quickly.

With a little research you can find out who is the best person to pitch your article to on large websites. On blogs, it may be the owner of the blog. How do you reach them?

Think about e-mails. Most of us have e-mail addresses like name@domain.com. If that blogger's name is Jeff, his e-mail is probably jeff@thiswebsite.com.

This is just a guess, but it's a good one. With some digging you can find out who to pitch. All this information is available online. Getting articles featured on large websites starts with deep, strong content.

After that it's about pitching to the right editor. They are the ones who decide what gets published or rejected.

Look at the image. We did some of your research for you. It's a list of editors at the *Huffington Post*. Look at their names and use the e-mail tip we just gave you. *Huff Post* editors' e-mail addresses will end in @HuffingtonPost.com.

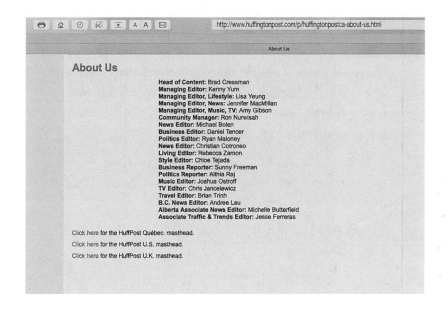

STRUCTURE YOUR PITCH

Kimanzi used to pitch pretty horribly. He used the "flattery" technique. This usually goes something like this:

> Hello so and so,
>
> I'm a huge fan of your blog. The content is great. I would love to give back by writing a guest post for your audience. Do you take guest posts?

Kimanzi used this format all the time with mixed results. First, the blogger sees right through this. They know you want exposure to their audience so the flattery and giving-back line seems fake to them.

A better approach is honesty, with something to back up what you're saying. Here's a better structure.

Hello so and so,

I'm a fan of your website. My favorite article is "Name a specific article that has helped you." I have written a guest post that speaks to your audience, which is at the bottom of this e-mail. (Bloggers *hate* attachments. Send the post in the body of the e-mail.)

Here are some samples of my work on these websites (name a few places you've guest posted and hyperlink the articles).

Thank you,

Your name

Then paste the article or articles. Another great strategy is to post three topics you want to write about, then bullet-point what each of those posts would be about.

The blogger can then decide which ones he or she likes. By listing three, if she or he doesn't like one or two, there are other options. They know best, and will tell you what works best for their website.

Use this same structure for large websites like the *Huffington Post* when you pitch the right editor.

That's it. If you want to get your work on a large website that can dramatically increase your audience, use the following steps:

1. *Do your research.* Who should you pitch? What is the best article to write? How much research did you put in the article? These questions have to be answered if you're going to successfully land a big guest post.

2. *Dig deeper.* Write from your heart. Get past the normal fluff and write about the topics most

people will be afraid to write about. Your post should strike a nerve and educate at the same time.

3. *Figure out the best approach.* Figure out whom to pitch to and what about. Do your research and find the person who can make it happen.

4. *Have the right structure.* Don't try to land your post with flattery. Let your research and content speak for itself. Show your past work to prove what you've got.

You can so do this, and the results will be life-changing! We don't mean to beat a dead horse, but Kimanzi has seen some game-changing results writing for large websites.

You build credibility that extends far beyond that website. You grow your e-mail list, social media presence, and get more business from these large websites. Not that many people do it, and these websites have tons of traffic, so the competition won't matter.

CHAPTER 9

EFFECTIVE PODCAST STRATEGIES

Navid Moazzez wanted to grow his online business to expand his impact and influence. He did not have a lot of resources to travel far and wide to attend overpriced events or purchase premium trainings. Navid lives in Stockholm, Sweden. It would have been easy for him to get discouraged.

Instead, he followed similar strategies that many other entrepreneurs use. He had a blog with reasonable traffic. He had a moderately successful podcast with great guest interviews that were helping his network increase. His e-mail list was growing little by little. He seemed to be doing everything right, but he was only achieving minimal results.

Navid believed that the next thing his business needed in order to grow was an event. Unfortunately, events can be expensive to organize and implement. Most people are disheartened by the costs needed to create a compelling event—especially one that would propel a brand to the next level. Navid realized he was not ready to arrange a live, in-person event. However, he could manage a virtual event.

Listen to Navid talk about this story in the following interview: http://starvethedoubts.com/navid.

VIRTUAL SUMMITS

A virtual summit is an online conference. The idea is not new. Online summit events are not only successful; they are very profitable, as well. Not everyone has the budget to travel, get hotels, and pay for costly events. The virtual summit is the perfect solution for the business owner who wants to experience high quality presentations from the comfort of his or her office or home, or anywhere a laptop, tablet, or mobile device will allow.

Navid had some great connections built through his podcast interviews and generous relationships with fellow members of his online community. He knew he could leverage these connections to create the Virtual Branding Summit. Navid got to work. He was a one-man gang. He quickly realized that putting together an online event on his own would require working smart, and not harder.

He learned the basics of what he needed to know. He also discerned that it would be easier for him to prerecord sessions and presentations instead of attempting to host them live during the actual event.

Navid joined together over eighty experts from various niches. He collaborated to create a symphony of interviews and sessions with friends, colleagues, and new connections. It took several months to pull everything together. The prerecorded interviews and sessions were structured just like an event or conference. Each day of the summit offered various sessions from relevant experts. He launched the Virtual Branding Summit and it was very successful, as anticipated.

The event was free for anyone who was willing to register with an e-mail address. Registered attendees received free access to each session, which were released for forty-eight hours. They had the option to purchase lifetime access and additional bonuses for $97. Navid offered affiliate programs to the presenters. They had the opportunity to offer the Virtual Branding Summit to their e-mail lists and receive a 50 percent commission for anyone who purchased. This compelled many of the experts to share the online conference with their networks.

Navid also created custom "I'm Speaking" images and gave them to the various presenters of the online conference. A large majority of the guests shared the custom images on their various social media channels, primarily for social proof reasons. (Think about it: Wouldn't you want friends and family in your network to know you were presenting or featured at an event?) The images were shared all over various social media networks. This bought a lot of attention to the Virtual Branding Summit. The result? Navid had thousands of people opt in to attend the event by signing up for his e-mail lists. He also had hundreds of people purchase the lifetime access and special bonuses. The event was a massive success and a major eye-opener for Navid.

Navid's event proved that a lot of people are interested in events with various sessions and speakers. With the exception of a few live webinars, his sessions were prerecorded interviews and prerecorded presentations that solved specific branding problems and provided lots of value.

What do events have to do with podcasting?

Podcasts are prerecorded and typically provide lots of value. What if you could leverage your audio or video interviews and the monologue presentations that were initially intended for your podcast to create a virtual conference? Could the perceived value of your virtual conference help launch your podcast with greater visibility and kick-start the growth of your e-mail list?

What if you could repurpose previous episodes of your existing podcast? What if you could bundle some of the best interviews and shows, and structure them like a conference? What if you marketed them as an online audio or video event? Would the strategic bundle of episodes and shows be perceived as more valuable if it were presented as an event instead of just another podcast? Could you offer access to the event simply for e-mail addresses? Could you offer special bonus and PDF guides (which are repurposed show notes) and potentially charge for the added access? Food for thought.

AUDIO BLOGS

Bloggers may not have an interest in podcasting, but they should. They could easily repurpose their content into an audio blog. This would greatly increase the visibility of their core message. The podcast app is now available on every Apple device. Apple CarPlay is accessible in new vehicles and allows drivers to listen to podcasts instead of the same old satellite or terrestrial radio. Stitcher Radio's partnership with General Motors has also democratized podcast consumption for the daily automobile commuter.

How easy is it for bloggers to repurpose their content to an audio blog?

It can be done 100 percent from a mobile device for free. You can pick up an amazing free PDF guide over at http:// audioblogstrategy.com.

CHAPTER 10

GETTING BOOKED ON TV

The New York Times estimates that the average American watches five hours a day of TV. It's also estimated that morning TV shows (http://www.mediabistro.com/tvnewser/category/morning-show -ratings) get 13 million daily viewers. Although 2.5 billion people will be online today, people still watch and give weight to TV. It's the equivalent of having a traditionally published book.

At the end of 2012, Kimanzi's business had taken off. It was generating income, but he was looking for ways to put a cherry on top of the cake. A friend suggested he book an appearance on some local morning shows. He taught me a strategy we're going to teach you about.

Here's what you should understand. It's not easy to get on TV, but morning shows have to air a wealth of good content, and do it every day. They are always looking for interesting pitches, and they don't want to miss a story.

When Kimanzi finally got on some morning shows in late 2012, his local business exploded. He got consulting work, coaching clients (although he didn't really think of it as coaching because he had no clue what he was doing), and people attending his live events. TV also helped him get better shelf placement for his book when it came out in May 2013.

Writing for large websites, getting booked on podcasts, and social media marketing are great ways to build an audience and promote a product. TV, however, is an incredible way to get exposure in front of millions of people. It's an original way of marketing because how many people do you know get booked on TV? We don't need to convince you of the value of this strategy, so let's talk about how to do it!

Start by targeting the weekend morning shows at your local TV stations. Always start local. We prefer local because that's where you know what's going on and probably have a connection.

Target local TV stations.

Start by targeting the weekend shows. They aren't watched as much as the weekday morning shows, so they're always willing to experiment. They also have an excessive amount of time to fill, so they're always looking. The thing to understand is that they fill slots, and a normal slot is three to five minutes. That's not a lot of time for you, but it's enough to make a good impression and have something to leverage the heck out of.

Choose a topic.

Identify what you're going to talk about on the show. You have three choices. It can be a current event going on where you live, a problem that has been going on for a while, or a general problem in our society. Here's an example of each.

1. *Current event.* A GMO moratorium initiative is being decided on by voters in Maui. Kimanzi could contact a morning show and pitch that

he would be a good guest to talk about this issue because of an article he wrote for the Huffington Post about the debate (http://www.huffingtonpost.com/kimanziconstable/watching-the-GMO-debate-a_b5979186.html). That would be his leverage to get on the show.

2. *Ongoing event.* Hawaii has a huge homeless problem (see http://www.civilbeat.com/topics/hawaii-homelessness/), and Kimanzi could pitch an appearance by taking an opposing view. Everybody talks about the problem, but he could offer a realistic and unique solution.

3. *General problem.* There are 3.5 million homeless people in America. Kimanzi could point out the lack of funding for homelessness while nearly $4 billion was contributed in campaign contributions in the recent elections (see http://www.huffingtonpost.com/ 2014/11/04 /2014-election-spending_n_6100894.html and http://www.studentsagainsthunger.org/page/hhp/overview-homelessness-america).

Before you read this and get on edge about the politics, look at the point we're making. Kimanzi learned the hard way not to talk about politics, so please don't have that be the takeaway. We only bring it up because it would be a powerful pitch. TV shows like airing a segment that gets people talking—positively or negatively. There are all kinds of things going on in your community and in America that you could pitch to a show. Use those events as your gateway to getting on TV.

Kimanzi always tries to give more than his opinion. In his research, he found some stats on what TV appearances have done for some restaurants (www.grubstreet.com/2011/10/restaurant-tv -appearance-impact.html). They all experienced their businesses doubling. OK, let's talk about where we are. Tim Ferriss credits his TV appearances as a big part of why his books hit *The New York Times* best-seller list (http://fourhourworkweek.com/2007/08/06/ how-does-a-bestseller-happen-a-case-study-in-hitting-1-on-the -new-york-times/). After one appearance on a morning show, Kimanzi added $4,000 in revenue.

We don't need to convince you of the value of a TV appearance. So let's continue.

Contact the associate producer.

The associate producer is the person in charge of finding good content. He or she has the authority to book you. The best time to reach the associate producer is between 10:30 p.m. and 2:00 a.m. They are starting their shift at that time and aren't as busy. If you wait, they'll be doing a thousand things and won't have time to talk.

Call them. On the phone. They get hundreds of e-mails, so your pitch will get lost in the chaos if you try to e-mail. Since they don't want to miss any stories that could be huge later, they always answer the news line. Always. Get the number from your local station's website (http://fox6now.com/contact) and call during those hours.

Be *brief!* Associate producers are super busy and don't have time to hear a long story. You have five minutes max to pitch. Give the pitch about the topic, and then tell him or her why you're the right person to talk about this topic. Leverage everything in your arsenal.

Don't tell them you're launching a book or something like that. If the producer suspects your motive is self-promotion, he or she will hang up. Show that you're going to add value and have clear takeaways, and when you get on the show, do just that. You have five minutes to convince that producer that your topic is relevant and that you're the right person to talk about it. If you want to be successful, you have to believe it!

Leverage that appearance.

You're on TV! How many people can make that claim? Be sure to dress well and smell good. Talk clearly. You only have a short amount of time, but don't talk so fast that people can't understand you. The goal of your appearance is to teach the viewers something; it's your job to be convincing.

People who saw you on TV will contact you, and businesses will reach out. You can also plaster the video everywhere! When you are submitting to speak at a conference, show the video. When you're trying to book consulting at a company, show the video. Leverage is what leads to income.

Before you launch your next book, product, or service, think about how a TV appearance can help. Leverage a local event and get yourself booked. Once you get one appearance, you will be viewed as the expert and producers will keep reaching out.

Does this really work? This is the question Kimanzi always asks himself when he reads something like this. This *does* work, and he has proof. We talked about leverage, and especially writing for larger publications. Kimanzi wrote an article for *Entrepreneur* magazine about up-and-coming podcasts (http://www.entrepreneur.com/article/237966).

Donald Kelly from the *Sales Evangelist* podcast (http://thesalesevangelist.com/podcasts/) and one of the podcasters in that article, went to his local CBS morning show and pitched a segment on why podcasting can benefit small business owners. He showed the article to prove that national media organizations are writing about this. CBS said yes, and brought on four of the podcasters from the article! The picture in this article is of those four podcasters after the TV morning show interview. They were able to leverage that article to get into their local paper. You can do this, too!

Remember, this is your year. Our goal is to help you build something that gives you freedom in every area of your life. We talked about hosting your own event. A TV appearance can fill that event pretty quickly. Use this strategy for success!

Are you going to try to get on TV?

CHAPTER 11

THE INS AND OUTS OF THE COACHING BUSINESS

The School of Coaching Mastery estimates that the average executive coach makes $325 per hour; the average business coach makes $235 an hour; and the average life coach makes $160 per hour. Kimanzi charges around $250 per hour. With over 2.5 billion people online daily, the amount of revenue made through coaching can be significant, and enough to quit your day job.

The money's there, but coaching isn't for everyone. More than that, most people have questions about how to start or grow a coaching business. Let's talk about how you can build a profitable coaching business as a part of your arsenal.

YOU CAN COACH

One of the biggest objections Kimanzi hears from people about starting a coaching business is the question of their credentials. We question our abilities at one point or another as to whether anyone should or will listen to us.

First, realize that the best training you can get is experience. If you have experienced something and triumphed through it, you've trained on the most important part of coaching. Learning something in a book or course is not the same as going through that situation in real life. If you have the experience, you can learn how to help people in the most effective way. You have what it takes to be a coach. Don't let haters keep you from making an impact on someone's life.

THE "FREE" CONSULTATION CALL

Kimanzi has given away 127 hours of free coaching since August 2011. Yes, that's an accurate number because he keeps track. One could look at all those hours as a lost opportunity, but he views it as his training on how to coach. He is a better coach because of that on-the-job training. However, Kimanzi doesn't recommend you do the same.

Generally speaking, people don't respect something as much when they get it for free. Our tip is this: *don't give away free coaching.* It's a strong statement, but we stand behind it.

We're not telling you to charge $200 an hour. We're saying that when someone has skin in the game, they're invested and are likely to take action on what you teach them. You can use a service like Clarity (https://clarity.fm/kimanziconstable) and charge a small amount, or tell people it costs $5 for a thirty-minute consultation session. The point isn't to make money.

You want to qualify your calls because those calls take up a valuable resource—*your time.* Qualifying calls separates those who are serious from those who aren't. Out of those 127 calls, about half of them were with people who were serious. Out of 127 hours of free coaching, seven became paid coaching clients.

A lot of experts will tell you to offer a free consultation call, with the premise that if someone wants to hire you, that call will give him or her the assurance needed. We can see their point, but we disagree. These calls are usually given to people who are not in the financial position to afford coaching but would love the free advice. In the end it's not the best use of your time. If you have a podcast or blog, you likely have tons of free content that you could direct them to.

Charging a small amount for these calls is not unreasonable and not out of most people's budgets. You can record these calls through a service like Free Conference call, and send the recording to them afterward so they can work on what you talked about. Everyone wins in that scenario.

Besides the money, there's an important psychological principle happening. If someone is going to chase a dream or make a big change, they have to change their mind-set. When they get a free session and possibly do something with the info, that doesn't change their mind-set.

When someone who doesn't have disposable income musters up a few bucks to learn something important to further their dream, they will take action, but it does something significant in their mind. In their mind they've "earned this," and they commit to the process of not giving up.

We get free content every day in the form of blogs, podcasts, and videos. If you want to know how to build a business, the information is all around. Yet many are stuck right now. Why? A small investment of money helps us focus. If you have ever paid for coaching, you know exactly what we're talking about.

Again, don't be offended if you've had free coaching. Read through what we're saying and use it in your business. Your time is worth something, and when someone pays even a small amount, he or she will respect you and the dream a lot more. If you operate a nonprofit or a ministry, ignore this advice completely.

When you're constantly giving away your time for free, no one will want to pay for that time. Why would they when they can get it for free? The way you make sales with your business is to show people that what you're selling is valuable. Constantly giving away your time isn't showing your value. Charge a small amount of money for your time and to help the mind-set of those you're talking to.

Remember, you might not be an A-lister yet, but that doesn't mean your time should be free. If you have experienced something and now teach that topic, your time is valuable and your audience should realize that. You're not teaching them theories; you're teaching what will help.

You may be thinking, "Why would anyone listen to me?" We live in a time of a lot of information. However, you would be surprised by what people know.

The topic you think has been covered enough, hasn't. If you are in this online space, then there are a lot of things we all know and get tired of hearing. People who aren't in this online space don't know what we see every day.

We know things because we read the same blogs, listen to the same podcasts, and watch the same videos. We're used to what we see every day, but the non-online person has *no* clue about these topics. You can still teach your topic to a *huge* audience that hasn't heard it or hasn't heard it in the way you teach it. This is why, with the right training, anyone can become a coach.

PRICING

OK, so we've established that you can coach, and that coaching can be a profitable revenue stream for you. Let's talk about money. Pricing for coaching can be handled in two ways.

Per-Month Pricing

In this model you charge a monthly fee for a certain period of time. The standard period is three months. In each month you have to decide how many calls or sessions you will offer. We have seen this vary from one call a month to one call a week.

The frequency of calls determines how much you'll charge. When in doubt, Kimanzi tells his clients to charge at least $97 an hour. That number is worth your time and is not out of reach for your potential clients. He's not a fan of the per-month model because people tend to shy away from something that feels like the expense won't stop.

Flat-Rate Pricing

In this model you charge a flat rate for your calls or sessions. This is the model Kimanzi uses for his coaching program. His customers have said they like this model because they can come and go as they please. Again, you decide what to charge per session. If you broke down Kimanzi's rate hourly, it's $250 an hour.

What should you charge? We're always going to tell you to test things out for yourself. What works for Kimanzi or someone else might not work for you. Try both systems and see what your customers respond best to. Testing is the key to success in any business.

THE STRUCTURE

So how the heck do you actually coach? Like pricing, coaching can be done in many ways—too many to list here. You can start simple with a Google Hangout (https://www.google.com/+/ learnmore/hangouts). It involves a video call with your client.

You can step it up and use a private video service like GoToMeeting (www.gotomeeting.com) or AnyMeeting (www .anymeeting.com). Each of these services has a free version. To record your sessions, you will have to upgrade to the paid version. With the paid versions you can record the sessions, share your screen, and take notes that will be automatically e-mailed to your client after the session. If you are going to use the free versions or a Google Hangout, you can use a Google Doc for notes between you and your client (https://docs.google.com).

These days Kimanzi uses Free Conference Call for his private and group coaching sessions. The service is free, but you can still record calls, share your screen, and do everything else you need to coach. The service even offers a transcription of your call for free. If you're looking for a cost-effective option, check this out.

There are many ways to monetize an online business, and coaching can be a lucrative one. In 2012 when Kimanzi's business started to take off, he got multiple requests for one-on-one coaching. For a long time he resisted because he's an introvert.

Kimanzi clearly remembers the day someone bought his $1,197 package when he launched his coaching business. He couldn't believe someone would pay him that much to coach them. Kimanzi, former bread guy from Wisconsin. Since then, he's had many $10,000 or more months. We're not telling you to brag, but to show you that you, too, can make significant income with your coaching business.

These days, Kimanzi is not taking any one-on-one coaching clients because of the different group programs he offers. You can decide to go one-on-one or with a group. Either way has amazing opportunities for your business.

MARKETING

The success of your coaching program will live and die by the marketing. Two of the best ways to market are word of mouth and your e-mail list. If you have helped someone or coached for free, ask her or him to refer your way someone who's looking for coaching. You'd be surprised by all the opportunities that are in your sphere of influence. You'll likely find your first or a new client by simply looking around.

The next place is your e-mail list. By now you know how big a fan we are of e-mail lists. The best way to sell to your e-mail list is with the soft sell. You're not trying to overwhelm your subscribers with an over-the-top Internet marketing sales pitch. The best way is to give them value, and simply mention that you have coaching for sale. Tell them that if they're getting value from the free stuff, imagine how good the paid stuff will be.

If your e-mail list has been consistently getting value, this will be a no-brainer for a few of those people on the list. The way you can give them extra value is by offering exclusive content. People on Kimanzi's e-mail list have told him they get value from his exclusive content on Saturdays. This softens the sell.

There are many ways you can market your coaching business. You can take out a Craigslist ad. When Kimanzi started his coaching business he took out a few Craigslist ads and got four clients in Milwaukee, where he used to live. By the same token you can take out an ad in your local paper or on your local news affiliate website. These are great for local clients.

You can pay for social media ads. Kimanzi has landed clients using Facebook ads. For a time, this was how he got all his coaching clients. Social sites have a vast amount of information about their users. When you pay for an ad, you can target those who see the ad. Facebook has options to target someone down to the cereal he or she eats. If you create an appealing ad and target the right people, they will click through to your website and check out the offer. If you make it appealing enough, they will buy without knowing you. Remember, these are people who are looking for what you offer.

Another way to market is through webinars. Offer a free webinar teaching something specific, and then offer your coaching services at the end of the webinar. If you create a compelling webinar, people will come. If they get value from the teaching, they will buy your coaching program.

To get even more bang for your buck, partner on a webinar with someone who has a bigger e-mail list. If you're in the online space, you've seen this happening. One person has a program or service and does a webinar with another person who has an e-mail list. Both parties split the profits.

Here's the thing: you don't need to partner with someone who has a big e-mail list. If you have an e-mail list of one hundred people, and someone you partner with has an e-mail list of two hundred people, that's three hundred people who could see your webinar. If you get forty people on the webinar, all you need is one person to buy. That's all you're shooting for, just one person.

Once you land one, then you focus on two, and so on. Too often we think we need to have ten people sign up for our program. If you get one person who buys your $1,197 program, that's a good chunk of money in your pocket. When you land a few of those each month, the income starts to overtake your day job. Focus on one person at a time rather than trying to land everyone!

CHAPTER 12

HOW TO SUCCESSFULLY SELF-PUBLISH

You've seen the A-listers do it, and you've seen the behind-the-scenes stuff because you were part of their launch team. You then tried their strategy for your book launch but didn't get the same results. Why?

The reason you didn't get the same results is because the A-listers already had large platforms before they launched. If you have a smaller platform, you're not going to be able to use their strategy and get the same results.

Many of us have experienced the bitter disappointment when we thought following the A-listers' blueprint would work for us but didn't. It's time we took a step back and realized what's going on and started using a strategy that fits our platform.

What is a small platform? The answer can vary, but for our purposes let's say anyone with less than 1,000 e-mail subscribers. Once you get to 1,000 you can really make significant income from your platform.

THE STRATEGY

1. *Understand your target audience.*

This is the key for everything you'll do. If you're not clear about who you're talking to, you'll never be able to figure out where they are and how to best reach them. Your book isn't for everyone. You have to get it in front of the people it is meant for—that's who will buy the book. Once you know your target audience, use that information to create a program they can't resist.

2. *Start building your platform ASAP—whether your book is out or not.*

- *Build your traffic through targeted guest posts.* The key to effective guest posting is being featured on sites that speak to your target audience. If you're talking about real estate but guest post on a leadership blog, what do you think the results will be? When we have a smaller platform we want to be featured in as many places as possible, but that's not a good strategy. Good guest posting is targeted and focuses on converting. Good guest posting is good for building back links to your site, which is good SEO. You can also write for large websites, which we went through a few chapters ago.

- *Focus on a difference-maker: conversions.* If you have twenty people on your e-mail list, focus on converting fifteen of those twenty people. Too often we focus on getting new people when the reality is most of our sales come from our existing audience.

- *Basic SEO.* Use strong headlines that are simple and have good key words. Mention your target key words in the first paragraph. Break up your content into chunks based on the key words.

- *Interviews.* BlogTalkRadio is your best friend when you're starting out or have a small platform. There are thousands of shows. Type in the key words related to your topic and see which shows are talking about it. Reach out to the hosts and highlight your story. Too often we want to jump in with why we're a good fit for a show, but let your story sell you. We all have a story to tell. It's the reason we do what we do. Highlight that. Subscribe to www.Radioguestlist.com as well. You will get shows that are looking for guests in your inbox every day.

- *Network with others in your industry.* We're not talking about trying to form a relationship with an A-lister in your industry. Too many people are trying that strategy. What I'm talking about is focusing on the third tier and building your network from the ground up. Years ago guys like Dave Ramsey, Dan Miller, and Michael Hyatt were friends who shared a passion for this industry. They were there for each other during the building years and built their network from the ground up. You have the same opportunity with those around you who might not have huge platforms but are building like you. What if you built together? Where would you be in ten years?

- *Social media.* Beyond just having accounts set
  up, maximize social media by deciding where
  you're going to be active and where you're going
  to be present. You only have a limited amount of
  time, and you can't be everywhere. Research the
  platforms your audience is most active on and
  spend that little bit of time you have there. That's
  where you're active. You're not active on the other
  ones but you post things from time to time. Give
  helpful tips and tricks on the non-active sites.
  We'll get more into social media later, but it's a
  great, free way to expose your book to the world.
  To build your platform through social media, give
  people a reason to come back. It has to be fresh
  and as original as possible. Don't just copy what
  you see the A-listers doing.

These are the basics, but again, if you're going to do this well
with a small platform, you have to focus on conversions. It's not
about building large numbers; this is about building strong, targeted leads that will turn into customers later. If you only have
one hundred people but eighty of them buy, you're in business.
That's our goal.

3. Adjust your expectations.

You're not going to build sustainable income on one book. Is
it impossible? No, but it's highly unlikely. Almost all successful
self-published authors have multiple books: Amanda Hocking,
John Locke, Josana Wilder, Joe Korath, Barry Eisler, and the
list goes on.

- *Realize your first book is just the beginning.* What
  we're building is a house, and the first book is the

foundation of that house. From this first book your goal is to springboard into more books and use the exposure from this book to launch other revenue streams. If you're self-publishing a book, I'm going to assume you're building something that you want to support you one day. The first book is just the beginning.

- *Launch other income streams.* Use the launch to not only sell a book but to launch other income streams in your platform. If you're a coach, tie in your coaching business. If you're a speaker, tie in your speaking business. There's so much exposure during your launch that it would be crazy not to convert it for more than just your book. If you have a small platform, this can be the key to creating something that actually supports you and your family. We're adjusting the expectations that this one book is not going to be it. We're realizing that we need more.

- *Set goals, not dreams.* Set a goal of one thousand books sold during launch week. One thousand books isn't going to make you rich, but it's a good starting point and it's decent income. You can use that number to springboard your book in Amazon's algorithm. That's the goal we want you to plan how to achieve.

- *Realize you have more than one chance.* If the launch doesn't go as planned for you, this isn't it. Self-publishing isn't a race, it's a marathon.

Determine that you're going to be in this for the long haul.

4. Create killer bonuses.

Typically we're told to create two or three things we can offer people. The idea that the more things, the more appealing buying the book seems is wrong. Instead of creating or offering ten things no one really cares about, create two or three things that are specific to your target audience and that they really want. Create things that blow your target audience's minds. These will be for the customers. The launch team (we'll get into what that is) will get a different set of bonuses. This is going to require some serious thought, planning, and a bit of work to create something killer.

5. Form a launch team.

You may have heard about this strategy, but like everything we've talked about, we're going to do it differently. We will form two launch teams: one will be bloggers who will review the book on their blog, share on social media, and write an Amazon review; the second team will be people who don't have a blog but will share on social media and write an Amazon review. The purpose of the launch team is to use the power of numbers and a bigger network. When forming the launch team, we won't just take anyone. They have to have a similar audience or something close. If they don't, we'll have them on the second launch team. This team will help let the world know your book and bonuses are out there and ready for people to get them.

6. Start teasing the book.

We're going to let your audience and the launch team's audience know it's coming, and we're going to remind them regularly but in fun ways, such as contests, giveaways, and so on. The sooner you start promoting, the better the book will do. Start making the book and your platform top-of-mind to potential buyers.

7. Prep the launch team.

The launch team should read the book and have their reviews and promotions set one week before the launch. We will help with the social media promotion copy by setting up quotes and things we want them to share. All they have to do is copy and paste. We will work on this two weeks before the book launches. We'll put some time into thinking about what to say, using good copy that appeals to your target audience. Prepping the launch team means really guiding them, letting them know exactly what you want them to do and when to do it.

8. Stack up guest posts and interviews.

We want as many as possible two weeks before the book launches and during the four days of the launch. Use every connection you have, and offer something for free to those willing to feature you, such as a free book to one of their audience members. Give people an incentive to feature you, and again, highlight your story. Go to BlogTalkRadio, as we talked about. Use Google to search for the right sites to guest post for. One key is to give yourself enough lead time. Guest posts on larger sites or interviews are usually set up weeks, maybe even months, in advance. When you're figuring out when to launch, plan enough time to work out the interviews and guest posts. They will be crucial. Reach out to anyone and everyone who speaks to your target audience.

9. Set up spots on local TV.

Despite the popularity of the Internet, people still watch TV. There's an untapped opportunity that we miss because we think it's impossible: being interviewed on our local stations. Think about how much content your local Fox or CBS affiliate has to fill. They're always looking for good content. The key is having a good hook, something that grabs attention or causes controversy. There's a strategy for how to get booked, which we shared a few chapters ago.

10. Launch the book over four days: Tuesday through Friday.

When we see A-listers launch a book, they usually use the whole week. The reason they're doing that is to make *The New York Times* best-seller list. That's not our goal—yet. For smaller platform launches, you don't need a full week, just three to four days max. Launch on a Tuesday and end on a Friday. Monday everyone is returning to work and starting their week, so they're not going to be thinking about your book. Once Saturday hits, people are thinking about how they will enjoy their weekend. Again, they're not going to be thinking about your book.

Tuesday through Friday is a solid four days when you have a chance to get your customers' attention. It's also shorter, so you can drive sales and possibly reach number one in a category on Amazon. I don't believe it will help your sales to claim the number one spot, but it's something good you can leverage to get interviews and guest posts on larger sites. We will promote hard during those four days and have the launch team do the same.

Use this strategy to rock your book launch. Use this as one tool in your arsenal.

CHAPTER 13

THE THIRD TIER

When Kimanzi started this business, he wanted to make connections with the top people online. There was and still is a ton of advice out there about how to connect with the first-tier people in your topic.

You're told to be persistent. You're told you have to stand out and offer to help an A-lister in some way. The only problem with that advice is that everyone else is seeing the same advice and trying to do the same thing.

Think about how much e-mail an A-lister gets a day. Kimanzi is not an A-lister, and he still averages over 300 e-mails a day. A-listers are getting hundreds, and a lot of those are people trying to connect with them.

We're not saying there's something wrong with that approach. Each of us has to decide what's best for us. We have to spend our time the way we think is important to us.

If your strategy is to get a top person in your industry to see your book, product, or service, and shout you out, it's not a good strategy. It would bring a lot of exposure quickly, but there's a better way. That's why we wrote this book.

Does it happen? Once in a while, but if you want this thing to support you there has to be a better strategy in place. If you read Kimanzi's blog, you know his goal is to be different from what everyone else does.

THE THIRD TIER

We want to tell you up front that this idea of the third tier isn't ours. Kimanzi first read about it from the guys at Fizzle (http://fizzle.co/sparkline/third-tier-theory-networking). We're telling you about it because it's a killer idea. The idea is instead of focusing on trying to get the attention of someone in the first tier, connect and make real relationships with someone in the third tier.

Think about Dave Ramsey, Michael Hyatt, and Dan Miller. They have been friends for over twenty years. They started out together and have helped promote each other throughout all these years.

They started in the third tier and built their own network. We don't know if they tried to reach out to any A-listers back then, but we do know that their network is very strong now.

If you're reading this, you have the opportunity to create a network just like theirs.

We know what you might be thinking—what are they going to sell us?

We have nothing to sell you. Thinking about this opportunity has Kimanzi's brain hurting. We have *so* much potential. If you can connect with other bloggers and people online in your industry and form relationships that are all about helping each other, the sky's the limit!

Reach out to those in your network, make real connections, and grow your online presence together. Even though you don't have a huge network and they don't have a huge network, your combined networks can grow together. What does this look like? Communicate with people who have a similar message to yours and get to know each other. Ask them what they're working on and see if you can help them promote that thing.

You can even form a mastermind group. Kimanzi is involved in an amazing mastermind group. He's learned so much and the members have helped each other build their networks together. You can do the same with those speaking to your target audience. When you come from a place of service, you'll reap huge rewards.

Talk about that person and eventually a group of people on your website and on social media. They'll talk about and promote you, and that's how you'll grow.

A lot of us are spreading a message of hope. Let's help each other out. Are you willing to help build a strong network together?

Think of the power that comes from building your own network from the ground up. Members of your group are on the same level and can help each other along the way. You'll become more than a network; you'll become real friends.

Instead of chasing influencers, build these real friendships. Find that group of people you can build with, and years later you will all be influencers.

Building relationships is powerful!

Kimanzi couldn't believe it was happening. His dream was becoming a reality. He got to the bread truck and was eager to finish his deliveries as fast as humanly possible. He had so many dreams and expectations. His book was being officially released to the world. The book came out that day and tanked. It continued to tank for the next five months. Kimanzi was depressed and tired of it all. He had some dark thoughts during this time and didn't even look at a computer for two weeks. So what made the difference? The amazing relationships in his life.

Three friends (one of which is Kimanzi's brother) were there for him during the best and worst of times. They told him life wasn't over. They told him to get back up and figure it out. They are one of the main reasons Kimanzi is living his dreams. Good (or bad) relationships can either make you or break you. They can be the key to success or lead you down the road to failure.

THE NEW REALITY OF RELATIONSHIPS

Back in the day, we would form relationships with people we met in person. In the reality of social media and the Internet, we form relationships in a brand-new way.

In the past four years, Kimanzi has had the honor of meeting many friends he initially connected with on the Internet. He even got to meet his friend Joe Lalonde at his book launch party. They met in the blogging world but had the chance to meet in person at a conference. Joe and his wife, Pam, drove up from Michigan and stayed with Kimanzi.

The new reality of relationships is that we're not limited by location or presence anymore. We can meet people from all around the world online and form great relationships that better our lives.

That's why we cringe when we hear people talk about social media and say, "It's just...." Social media is modeled after what it would be like interacting in person, with the only difference being you do it online. Those relationships can be just as real as in person and can even be better in some ways because you can help each other do so many cool and new things online.

When you want to spread a message or help someone go through an experience you went through, who better to help you spread that message than the people you have formed relationships with online?

CUT OUT NEGATIVE RELATIONSHIPS

Have you ever told a friend or family member about something you want to do to better your life and had that dream torn apart? Have they given you one hundred reasons why it won't work before you even try it?

These relationships will affect any change in your life in a negative way. You already have enough doubt and fear. Listening to this constant affirmation of those doubts and fears will lead you to fully embrace them and give up. If you want the best chance for success, you're going to have to cut the negative from your life, and that includes people. It doesn't have to be forever, but it will give you the best chance for success right now!

Relationships are important to your life and your success. Think about the relationships in your life. Are they right for life and your success right now? Be honest. If there are some changes that need to be made, make them today.

CHAPTER 14

HOW TO HOST YOUR OWN CONFERENCE FOR LITTLE OR NO MONEY

In the paid speaking world, there are three ways to make money. The first is speaking at conferences. When we think of a conference, we think of an event like Podcast Movement. However, these big events do not usually pay speakers. Because they're so popular, many speakers gladly come and speak for free.

If you want to make money speaking at conferences, your best bet is to speak at the conferences of industry associations. These industries could be health care, lawyers, auto, and so on. Speaking for these associations doesn't mean you have to talk about their industry. You can talk about topics to help their industry, and these are the topics they want to learn more about.

Kimanzi used to live in Milwaukee, next door to the huge speaking market of Chicago. He would regularly travel to Chicago to speak to health care professionals about how to better use social media, and he got paid a pretty penny to do it. Research the industry association meetings where you live, and send them a pitch. Those associations have plenty of money to pay you to speak. We'll get into this later.

The second way to book paid speaking is consulting at companies. Since Kimanzi has written a lot about this, he won't talk about it here. The third way to book paid speaking is to host your own event.

WHY HOST YOUR OWN EVENT?

Hosting your own conference is the ultimate goal of any speaker. You bring people to your event, where you control everything. You have a chance to make money by selling your products and services.

First, reframe what you think of as a conference. Think of your conference as a one- or multiple-day training event.

In this one-day training, you will teach how to do what you do, or the process you use for what you do. You can even make this a multiple-day event where you give a wealth of actionable material. Since this is training, your goal should not be to get five hundred people. You're looking more in the fifty-person range. You want this to be intimate so people see the value and you can control the crowd.

LOCATION AND EXPENSES

First, find a place to have the event. Kimanzi's first one-day training was at a local hotel in Milwaukee. It cost him $95 to rent a conference room that came equipped with a pulpit, wireless microphone system, chairs, tables, and everything else he needed.

Search around where you live for a place to rent that's affordable and central. You might even be able to negotiate the rate by bartering or offering free advertising for that place. Check

Craigslist or even put out your own ad. You'll be surprised how cheaply you can find a place to use.

You have the choice of whether to offer lunch at your event. If you do, increase the price. At Kimanzi's first event he had Cousins party subs and chips. The material taught attendees how to start an online business. It was from 9:00 a.m. to 5:00 p.m.

Ten people attended the event, and he grossed $970. He had paid $257 for food, the room, flyers, Facebook ads, a local paper ad, and juice. Got to have the juice. Right?

Even if you have to pay, this could be very cost-effective. If you hosted an event and it cost you $200 in expenses, all you would need is three people and you're profitable! Can you get three people? I'm very confident you can.

SPONSORS

The way you can host your event for free is to get sponsors. This is what Kimanzi did for his second event. He got a local print company to sponsor him—they cut him a check for $2,000 in return for advertising their business on all his materials and at the event.

There are companies where you live that would sponsor your one-day training. You just have to show them the value. Abbie Unger, one of Kimanzi's coaching clients, hosted her first event completely sponsored.

Our suggestion is to approach small- to medium-size companies. You want to be able to talk to a person (and not send a cold e-mail), and especially a person who can write a check. Offer to take this owner or manager out to lunch and give them the readers' digest version of your vision for this event. The key is showing them the value. How do you do this? The short answer is leverage anything you can.

If you have a decent social media following, tell them you'll be promoting their company on your platforms. If you have spoken before, use that. If you write for large websites, show them that. Large websites can be juicy leverage. Believe in yourself and the value you provide, and it will come through in your pitch. Realize that you're not asking for $10,000. You'll likely ask for $1,000 at the most. If you show him or her you will fill this event and advertise that company, this will be a no-brainer. Tell them they're getting in on the ground floor of what will be an annual event.

MARKETING

Whether or not you get a sponsor, you still have to market your event. Look at your calendar. Pick a date six months from now. Write the name of your one-day event on the calendar.

Six months should give you more than enough time to market, plan, and maximize your event. If you get a sponsor, you can use some of that money on Facebook ads and other social media. Since this event is where you live, it's also worth it to take out an ad in your local paper. People still read those!

A few off-the-wall ideas are Craigslist and Meetup. You can take out a free Craigslist ad telling people about your event. To get their attention, offer a free door-buster price. It can be something small, but people love free.

Meetup is a site where you can form groups that include people locally and from all around the world. You can form a group related to your event. Meetup's algorithm will send the people who would be interested your way. You can have the event clearly scheduled as people join your group.

Building a freedom business involves many components. One that appeals to many entrepreneurs is public speaking. We hope you've seen that hosting your own conference is not only a reality, but also something you should try at least once. Kimanzi is an introvert, so he knows what you fellow introverts are thinking, but this can be profitable and build your business.

Think about the math behind this. You host a conference that charges $97 a ticket. You can get the conference sponsored, which means everything you make is profit. If you don't, you can keep expenses down by renting a place for $100 to $150, and buying lunch and juice, which would cost close to the room. Let's be generous and say your expenses are $400. When you get five people, you're profitable, but what about beyond that?

What about when you get ten to twenty people? What if you hosted the same (or a different) event once a month? When you think about it that way, it becomes a serious source of income. Kimanzi has two clients who host a different event every month and earn $4,000 after expenses. Not bad at all.

THE EXTRAS

We've talked about making money from your event, but what about other ways to monetize? *This is your event,* meaning you can promote your other products and services to an audience that has already proven they're willing to spend money with you. That is the definition of a "hot lead."

We're not telling you to make your event a hype machine where you try to cram your other offerings down people's throats. What we are saying is that when you give over-the-top value, don't be afraid to mention other offerings that could benefit attendees.

You can set up a table that has your books, a one-sheet to book you to speak, and a one-sheet that explains your coaching program or group class. When you add value at your event, people will naturally want to know what else you offer. The income adds up.

Be sure to have a sign-up sheet for your e-mail list at the event. At the very least it's a good opportunity to add names of future customers. You can have a sign-up sheet or use a text-to-add program.

Many e-mail service providers now offer the option of opting in to your e-mail list through text messaging. Kimanzi uses MailChimp, and they offer it. (http://connect.mailchimp.com/integrations/text-to-join-for-mailchimp) It's very convenient to say "text hello to 555" and get people to sign up.

You can host your own event!

CHAPTER 15

HOW TO BOOK PAID CONSULTING GIGS

You may not realize it but the most profitable part of the speaking industry can be training at companies. Every day companies all around the world hire people just like you or independent contractors to train their employees on a wide range of topics.

Kimanzi started speaking in 2012 and spoke at thirty-six events that year. That year he made $16,233 from speaking. In 2013 he spoke at twelve events and made $22,000 from speaking.

In 2013 Kimanzi spoke at fewer events but more of those events were private training at companies. He did training at various companies where he lived in Milwaukee as well as companies in London and Paris.

Yes, you read that right. He was able to do training for companies internationally and they paid all of his and his wife's travel expenses. Speaking isn't his passion but traveling is, so he went. He and his wife had an amazing experience!

Many people who read Kimanzi's blog want speaking to be part of their business. If you look at most calls for speakers, you'll see that most events don't pay speakers. You can find paying events in specific industries but you're going to have to do some work to get booked.

For those of you who want to generate some speaking income a little quicker, training at companies can be your thing. Kimanzi is writing this on a very exciting day! A coaching client of his just landed his first contract to do training at a large car dealership. The cool thing is if he does well he has a chance to train for twenty other dealerships!

We want to teach you how to get contracts to speak at companies. We've already told you about the why, so now we will teach you the how. Our goal is for anyone who reads this to get his or her first contract within the next month! That is, if you want to, of course.

Training at companies can add some nice side income, and if you do it well, it can be your full-time income. Kimanzi's friend trains at companies 365 days a year and brings in some nice income.

START LOCAL

You may want to travel the world and see cool new places, but it always starts local. The first time Kimanzi did any training at a company it was at a local McDonald's.

A man owned three McDonald's restaurants in Milwaukee. Kimanzi would see him all over the city. This was in 2012, when social media was really starting to take off. Kimanzi went to his office and presented him with an offer. He didn't know anything about pricing back then, so he signed a contract for $500. It was the first money he ever made from speaking.

You want to start local because that's where you know people. Local is where you can form real relationships and have a chance to talk to someone who will listen. You can try to approach a company somewhere else but it will be a cold approach. Local means you know someone who knows someone, and they can get you in front of the right person.

You know what's going on where you live, so when you make your proposal, you can make it relevant to what's going on locally. Start by opening your eyes a little. What companies are around you that you can get in front of the president or owner? Look for smaller companies at first. It can be a local McDonald's franchise or a car dealership. Your aim is to find a place where you can talk to a decision maker.

Your homework is to make a list of three smaller companies that you can approach to train on your topic.

IDENTIFY THE PROBLEM

Once you've identified a local company you can approach, what problem are you going to help them with? For Kimanzi it was social media. He saw that the local McDonald's franchisee had a horrible social media presence.

The company's updates were inconsistent and most of their engagement was complaints from customers. Kimanzi put a presentation together showing the owner where he was missing out. He showed him the problem and offered a solution.

You can identify a problem for a local company in your area. The problem is likely something related to what you teach. If you teach real estate, you can train a local company on better ways to do certain real estate processes. This is going to require some thought, but you can probably identify a problem with a company where you live. Figure out what that problem is and the best way to fix it.

Next we'll talk about putting together that presentation and who to present it to. We hope you use this information to lock in some lucrative contracts that help your dream become a reality. There is so much opportunity waiting for you if you'll take it.

Do you want speaking to be part of your business? Can you think of a local company to approach?

If your dream is to get paid for speaking, consulting for companies can be a very profitable introduction into that market. In 2013, companies spent $39.3 billion paying consultants, according to *Business Week*.

That's a lot of money, and some of that could be yours if you can approach the right company. As we mentioned, the first training Kimanzi did at a company paid $500. It was low, but he didn't have to do much. His job was to keep up the franchisee's social media platforms and grow its presence.

The result was that the local McDonald's social media platforms grew by 26 percent, and customer complaints on social media decreased by 68 percent.

Kimanzi didn't make a ton of money on that contract, but the owner did connect him with several others business owners, which led to some serious money.

Flash forward to 2014.

Kimanzi's family moved to Maui on April 8. He had plenty of coaching business, but with the exposure he was getting from all the interviews, he was contacted by a company. The company had heard some interviews and seen Kimanzi's work. He was asked to come in and talk about an opportunity. He can't give all the details for legal reasons, but he walked out of that meeting with a pretty sweet offer.

Kimanzi sent the offer to his attorney, and they were able to negotiate a sweet contract! His job is to build this company's overall online presence. For every 1 percent Kimanzi grows its overall presence, he gets $1,000. He has been working on it for the past two months and has grown the company's presence 8 percent. Business is good!

Kimanzi doesn't want to brag, because he's really not any more special than anyone reading this. We want to share this to demonstrate that ordinary people like you can make serious money by teaching topics you love teaching. We hope you're excited, because the sky's the limit! Let's finish up.

CREATE A COMPELLING PRESENTATION

Once you've identified a problem that you want to help a company solve, it's time to lay it out in a presentation. It can be a PowerPoint or Keynote (for Mac users). The goal is to define the problem and the solution on slides.

You should have no more than ten slides, and each slide should have about six to ten words. It's better to have pictures and charts to illustrate what you're talking about.

The key to a good presentation is to get people to pay attention to you. If you have a bunch of words and bullet points on a slide, they'll be reading those instead of paying attention to you.

The slides are only meant to complement what you're saying. They should give a visual to your words. Put together a compelling presentation that outlines the problem and the opportunity for fixing that problem.

You'll be giving this presentation to one person at first. Depending on how much authority that person has, you might have to give it to a group of people in that company. Be prepared either way.

A great presentation is well-practiced but doesn't sound rehearsed. If you want some guidance on good presentations here are a few resources:

- TED Talks (www.ted.com).

- One of the best books we've read on presentations is *Resonate* by Nancy Duarte (http://resonate .duarte.com/#!page0).

- If you want to create good slides, Duarte's other book, *Slide:ology*, is killer (http://www.duarte .com/book/slideology/).

This is everything you need to put your presentation together and rock it. After that you lock in that contract!

GET IN FRONT OF THE RIGHT PERSON

This is what it all comes down to. This is the make-it or break-it moment. If you're going to land a contract with a company, you have to find the right person to pitch. This is going to require some good old-fashioned research.

You can start online with that company's website. There's usually a list of the top management. Find the senior person who is a step lower than the CEO. An even better way is through word of mouth.

If you know someone who knows someone at the company, that can improve your chances. If you can see the owner somewhere else, you will have success.

The goal is to figure out whom to pitch. For Kimanzi it was meeting that owner. For his client it was the same thing. Research and find that person.

When you figure it out, be brief. We suggest trying to get them on the phone or meet in person. That's a better option than a cold e-mail. You'll have a better chance of closing if they can see you or hear your voice.

Outline the problem you've seen and tell them about the opportunity. Your whole pitch should be no more than fifteen minutes, unless you're sitting down to lunch or in their office.

Your main goal is to get a meeting. When you get that meeting, rock your presentation and lock in that contract. If they say no, move on. Don't view it as a rejection.

Expect to get some nos. Expect some people to blow you off. That's just the nature of the thing. Get back up and figure out what other companies you can pitch. It's a numbers game. For every yes, there will be a ton of nos. Focus on the yesses, because that's what makes this thing support you.

CHAPTER 16

HOW TO BOOK PAID
SPEAKING ENGAGEMENTS

Who wouldn't want to be a worldwide speaker? Can you imagine traveling to cool, exotic places, and getting paid for it? This sounded like a crazy fantasy to Kimanzi, too, until it happened! Here's the backstory.

For twelve years Kimanzi was absolutely miserable. He dreamed of a better life, but didn't do a single thing to make that life a reality. The one thing that really depressed and angered him was his work; he was in a job he thought about quitting daily.

After some changes at work, things went from bad to worse. Kimanzi told himself enough was enough. He was going to finally make those changes. It was almost one year later when things at work came to a boiling point, and he had to take action or go nuts.

He thought about becoming a writer, but how could he really make a career out of that? It was after two weeks of writing that he ran across the story of a woman named

Amanda Hocking (http://www.guardian.co.uk/books/2012/jan/12/amanda-hocking-self-publishing).

To make a long story short, she sold 1 million copies of her three e-books in eight months.

Kimanzi clearly remembers the day he'd finally had enough. He cried. He paid for the book to be put together and kept promoting. The day the book came out he rushed through work, ran home, and logged on to Amazon to see the sales. Can you guess what he saw?

Yep, you're right. He didn't sell a single copy of his book! He was confused. So many people had told him they would buy the book. What was going on?

In the end he has sold over 86,000 copies of his two e-books, and he did it without spending a single dollar on advertising. He ended up signing a four-book deal with a publisher: http://www.soundwisdom.com/2012/05/kimanzi-constable-signs-publishing-agreement-with-sound-wisdom/.

Once the book deal was officially announced, Kimanzi knew the next natural step was to speak.

THE STRATEGY

Kimanzi wanted to know how he could get paid and see the world. He went to something he had used many times before: Google.

He searched the term "call for speakers 2012" and got millions of results. He narrowed his search and thought about what he could talk about from his experiences.

He thought about the fact that he had experience selling e-books online, only using social media, so he searched for "call for speakers 2012 social media."

That term brought him to the first paid event he officially booked (http://the-bam.com/bam/more_speakers.html) in Huntington, West Virginia. He leveraged the fact that he had successfully sold e-books through social media and had done it so well that he got a book deal. The organizer said yes!

Once Kimanzi got the first deal, he hit the ground running. He started reaching out to people he had networked with at a Brendon Burchard conference.

Reaching out to those contacts is what led to the booking of Kimanzi's second event: WordCamp 2012 in New York. He told the organizers he had booked the conference in West Virginia and that he had a book deal.

During this time he continued searching Google, and when he found an event that met his criteria, he sent the conference organizer a formal speaker proposal.

As he searched, he picked up one valuable tip: narrow his search even more. As he found events he thought would work, he figured out that some of them were old or the call for speakers had already expired.

Kimanzi went to the advanced settings in Google and switched the time to search for only results from the past month. Sometimes he wanted to get fresh events, so he changed the settings to the past week. He got really slick and started setting Google alerts for certain events he was curious about. He would wake up every day and have events to send proposals to. It's an excellent little tool.

KIMANZI'S SPEAKER TEMPLATE

Before we continue, we want to show you Kimanzi's speaker's template. He gets tons of requests to see this, but you're one of the first.

Name, Title, Experience

My name is Kimanzi T. Constable; I'm a writer/ blogger/author/social media expert.

My website is http://kimanziconstable.com.

Last August I self-published my first e-book, and to date it has sold a little over 86,000 copies. I have also signed a book deal with *Sound Wisdom.*

Here is the official press release: http://www .soundwisdom.com/2012/05/kimanzi-constable -signs-publishing-agreement-with-sound-wisdom/.

I have been featured on some of the largest websites in the world:

http://www.48days.com/2012/02/23/stop/

http://goinswriter.com/platform-now-what/

http://michaelhyatt.com/the-most-important-hour -of-the-day.html

I have done several interviews and podcasts (you can see them on my About page).

Writing

I'm a contributing writer for the *Huffington Post.*
I'm a contributing writer for The Good Men Project.
I'm a contributing writer for *Entrepreneur* magazine.
I'm a contributing writer for MindBodyGreen.

Contact Information

kconstable29@gmail.com

Phone: 414-916-4614

Speaking Engagements

May 31, 2012, I spoke at the Bam Social Media Conference 2012 in Huntington, West Virginia.

June 9-10: I spoke at WordCamp 2012 NYC.

June 30-July 1: I spoke at WordCamp 2012 Reno, Nevada.

July 21-22: I spoke at WordCamp 2012 Sydney, Australia.

July 28-29: I spoke at WordCamp 2012 Arkansas in Fayetteville, Arkansas.

August 18-19: I'm booked to speak at WordCamp Grand Rapids in Michigan.

August 24-26: I'm booked to speak at WordCamp Albuquerque in New Mexico.

September 15: I'm booked to speak at WordCamp Los Angeles in California.

October 17: I'm booked to speak at the Hawaii Social Media Summit in Oahu.

November 10-11: I'm booked to speak at WordCamp Kenya in Nairobi.

Session Proposal and Brief Description

I would have a session on one of the following topics:

How to Start and Market a Profitable Online Business through Social Media: Just based off your life experience and knowledge, you are one of three

151

types of expert. You can take that expertise and knowledge, combined with our modern tools and technologies on the Web, and create an online business that gives you a life of freedom and value.

My session will teach you which type of expert you are, what tools and technologies work best for you, and how to bring it all together and create products and services that change people's lives.

I will teach you how to create this web-based business for little or *no* cost. I will then teach you the key to marketing on the Web and in social media.

I will show you how I used these strategies to create a six-figure-a-year online business. I will show you how I self-published two e-books and sold over 86,000 copies, got a book deal, became an international speaker, and created products and services that are used worldwide. These aren't great theories; I have actually done this and can teach you to do it!

The Power of Your Story through Social Media: With over 2.5 billion people online every day, there has never been a bigger or better audience to market your business or spread a message. There are also many people trying to get people's attention, like you. How will you stand out? How will you be heard above all the noise?

My session will teach you the best way to market your business or message: the power of story. I will teach you how to shape your story, along with the tools and tricks to use your story on the Internet and in social media. I will teach you the most effective way to identify your target audience and how to use your story to speak directly to them.

I will show you how I used my story to self-publish two e-books and sell over 86,000 copies and to become an international speaker and life coach. You *can* do this.

Compensation

My fee is $3,000.00 plus expenses. I fly exclusively through Delta airlines and stay at Hilton hotels. For this amount I will make sure you get an over-the-top experience for your conference.

I would be honored to speak at what will be an amazing conference. I believe my contributions can help.

I'm young and have energy and know what it takes to keep a crowd engaged and active. I can teach them how to leverage exposure in social media to get partnerships and sponsorships. I can help them learn how to use social media to accomplish things they've only dreamed about!

Give me a chance and I will show your audience what's possible with a little hard work!

Thank you for time,
Kimanzi T. Constable

This is the template Kimanzi sends out to event organizers. The one thing to make clear is your fee. We've seen so many speakers focus on booking the events that they neglect to mention the fee. They try to go back and ask for a fee, but by then the damage is done. Make it clear up front. If they can't afford to pay, then you'll know right away. .

BACK TO THE STRATEGY

Just by using Google, Kimanzi was able to book conferences in Mumbai, India; Oahu, Hawaii; and California. Through networking at an event he attended, he booked conferences in Reno, Nevada; Sydney, Australia; New Mexico, and Nairobi, Kenya. In the end, he spoke at events in eight states and three countries in 2012.

Here are a few tips to use.

PREP WORK

Before you start pursuing speaking events, set up a formal speaker proposal. What should a formal proposal have in it? (You've already seen Kimanzi's.) Start with a little biographical information. Use your story to make it more appealing. A personal angle makes organizers feel as though they can identify with you. Make it personal in a way that's relevant to the event you're trying to book. This might mean that you have multiple templates.

At the beginning, tap into the power of story. Story is powerful and helps people understand you better. Next, think about what have you done. Where have you spoken? Have you written a book? What could you list as an accomplishment that would be relevant to an event organizer?

Have plenty of links to your previous speaking events or videos of you speaking, as well as to whatever accomplishments you list. Event planners want to see proof of what you have done, and to see if you can do what you say you can do.

If you don't have anything to point to, then it's time to get to work. Is there somewhere you can speak just to get some video and testimonials? Many first-time speakers like to join the National Speakers Association (http://www.nsaspeaker.org).

You can also do things such as speak at your local library, at your local chamber of commerce, or at a work event. The point is to get out and speak, record the video, and get testimonials. If you really put your head together, you can find somewhere to speak and get what you need.

Have your contact information readily available with multiple ways to contact you. List the topics you want to speak about, and go into detail about what the sessions will be about and why they'll be amazing.

Focus on what the audience will take away from your talk. Event organizers are looking for presentations that have definite takeaways for their audience.

Have your pay requirements structured. Are you going to take a lump sum? Are you going to get a base and expenses? It's important to determine up front how and when you'll get paid.

When Kimanzi spoke at international events, he asked for half of his payment up front through PayPal. He didn't know much when he first started, but he knew he didn't want to fly halfway around the world and not get paid! State your fees and payment requirements clearly up front. This is a mistake that most newbie speakers make repeatedly.

In some cases you will have to pay for your accommodations up front and get reimbursed at the event. These are the kind of things you should sort through as you're searching for the right event.

Finish with why you would be a good fit as a speaker. Emphasize how much energy you have and how you'll get the crowd active.

This will be a template that you send to multiple types of events, so try to make it general. If you really want to be ahead of the game, you can have multiple proposals for different types of events. It might take more time up-front, but can save you time later.

What if you don't have previous experience? We hate to say this but it's the truth: if you haven't spoken anywhere then you're going to have to build your portfolio by speaking at some events for free. Get a couple under your belt so that you can leverage them to get paid events.

Even though they're free, you have to go above and beyond and have the best presentation they've ever seen. Use that footage to feature your talents. Special note: wherever you speak, for free or not, make sure you get recommendations from everyone, such as people in the audience, the organizer of the event, and whoever you can get a testimonial from. Organizers love to see recommendations from someone other than you!

If you have a book, product, or service, you can make some of your expenses back by selling it at the back of the room. You have to be really careful here. If you make your presentation a sales pitch, people will be completely turned off. No one wants to sit through a sales pitch.

NETWORKING AND LEVERAGE

When you're at free events, just attending a conference, or meeting influential people, network with them and find out if they have any hot leads.

Form honest, mutually beneficial relationships. The goal isn't to use anybody. Just be honest and up front about your goals. The best relationships are built with honesty. There's a tremendous opportunity at conferences to form amazing new relationships. You just never know who you're going to meet and where that will take you.

Kimanzi is a shy person naturally, but he's learned the value of meeting people. Heck, that's how he met his publisher. When you do anything that would interest an event organizer, leverage that for all it's worth. You have to be outgoing. Hand your business card to everybody you meet. You never know who that person is or what he or she can do for you.

FIGURE OUT YOUR STRATEGY

When Kimanzi first started searching through Google and began networking, he planned out exactly how he would go about it. He determined that he would send out two speaking proposals to conferences a day, five days a week. That sounds like a lot, but he wanted to be a speaker badly. He knew that to increase his chances of getting booked, he had to get his name and bio out there to as many people as possible.

So every weekday, even though it seemed boring and time-consuming, Kimanzi sent out proposals. It felt as though he wasn't making progress because he didn't hear back from any conferences for a long while, but eventually it paid off in a big way. You may have more time or more patience, so you might decide to send out two a week. Find the number that works for you and start consistently sending out proposals.

It took a few weeks, but after Kimanzi sent out the initial proposals, organizers started getting back to him with questions. That's the first step! You can start getting booked as a speaker. It will take some planning and some hard work. The key will be once you get that first opportunity, you have to prove you're worth it. So get out there and make it happen today!

Could it really be as simple as this? Yes! It's not hard to find events and get in contact with the organizers. The hard part is convincing them that you're a good fit, but we have confidence in you!

SOME HELPFUL WEBSITES

There are several places to start looking for speaking opportunities and get great advice.

Lanyrd

One of the main places Kimanzi looks for events is this website: http://lanyrd.com/. It has a huge database of events all around the world. The only hitch is that you'll have to do some sorting through to find the events you're looking for. Kimanzi likes how it breaks it down by category and calendar.

You can track events and create a profile with your information for event organizers to see and possibly book you. This website is also connected with social media. When you book an event or want to book an event, it will be visible on social media networks.

Google

Google (https://www.google.com) can be great to get an event or announce to the world, and by extension other event organizers, that you're speaking somewhere.

We've covered this a few times in this chapter, but Google is an amazing resource. It has everything you need to find the types of events you want to speak at. Like the other website we mentioned, there will be some sorting through to do.

There have been times in the past when Kimanzi had to go to page twenty before he found an event he thought would work. If you're committed to launching your speaking career, you'll have to put in some work. Google can help you find some amazing events. At the time of this writing, Kimanzi just booked an event in Jerusalem, Israel, that he found through Google.

National Speakers Association

The National Speakers Association (http://www.nsaspeaker
.org) is a great place to become a better speaker. It's also a great
place to network with other people who are trying or have done
what you're looking to do with speaking. You will be able to make
connections that lead to your first event.

OTHER PLACES TO LOOK

There are other places to book speaking engagements that are
more local.

Chamber of Commerce

Every city has a chamber of commerce. You can find out
who's in charge, when and where they meet, and what they're
talking about each month.

There will be times when they meet that will be a great opportunity for you. Talk to the person in charge and show him or her
how you and your talk would be a good fit. The key is to have
great content and be confident that you can deliver.

Speaking at your local chamber of commerce will lead
to many new and amazing opportunities. These meetings
are for business owners, so speaking in front of them will be
great exposure.

Business owners from all over your state will see you have
something they need for their business. They can hire you to
speak at their companies, retreats, or events. If you get in, maximize this opportunity by networking afterward.

Industry Associations

Certain industries get together for best practices meetings. It could be the food association, a leadership association,

or whatever. The point is, this is a great place to get in front of industry leaders and open doors.

The cool thing is that even if it's an industry that you might not necessarily target, they may be discussing a topic you are qualified to talk about.

Kimanzi spoke at a medical industry association meeting, a place he wouldn't be normally talking. However, they were talking about social media, which Kimanzi speaks about all the time. When he found the event through Google, he sent out his proposal and got the event.

Even though it wasn't his normal scene, he was able to speak at a great event. He knocked it out of the park and booked a few other events. Sometimes you have to look outside the box, and you'll have a full schedule in no time.

Local Meet-ups, Libraries, and Other Events

There are a lot of other places to speak; you could probably add dozens to this list. The key is to find them and show whoever is in charge that you would be a good fit. These events will usually be local, but can build your portfolio and add a little income to your pocket. The key is to figure out what your requirements are and state those up front.

There are also companies looking to bring in other experts, and you can be that expert. They are looking for high-quality training and are willing to pay high-quality dollars. Events and opportunities are everywhere. Just keep your eyes open.

Paid speaking can and should be part of your business-building efforts. You can generate income and travel the world. Use these tips to create another level in your business. Use it to help you create a life of freedom.

PART FOUR

HOW TO LEVERAGE

CHAPTER 17

ONE DOOR LEADS TO MANY MORE

We want to give you one valuable tip that Kimanzi just learned. We won't keep you in suspense: *look beyond the little pond we all seem to be swimming in right now.* Learning this tip has helped open so many doors.

The number one way Kimanzi built his audience is through guest posting. One guest post for Michael Hyatt in 2012 put him on the map.

He's a guest-posting evangelist. He tells his clients to do it, and if you've been reading his stuff for a while you've seen him talk about it. We have talked about it throughout this book.

When we talk about guest posting on larger websites, who comes to mind? You might think of Dan Miller, Michael Hyatt, Jeff Goins, Pat Flynn, Amy Porterfield, and so on. You can probably list fifteen to twenty websites.

Here's the problem: if you are thinking about trying to guest post on those websites, how many other people do you think are, as well? More than that, we all read those same websites. How much overlap is there between those audiences?

For a long time Kimanzi was one of those people, until a few weeks ago. He started writing a guest post. After the post was done, he started to think about where it would fit. He thought those usual places would be great, but wondered what else was out there. He started looking at really large websites.

Kimanzi looked to see if they take contributors and was surprised to find most large news and information websites do. He submitted that article to the *Huffington Post* and, with the nudging of a friend, it got in front of the eyes of Arianna Huffington. As you know, that post went live and has blown Kimanzi's mind to the possibilities. He did the same thing with another guest post, and it went live on The Good Men Project, which gets 2 million visitors a week. This post has been shared over 100,000 times!

Kimanzi has since started writing for a few more places: *Huffington Post, Entrepreneur* magazine, The Good Men Project, MindBodyGreen, and Business Insider. What results has he seen? He has added 19,000 e-mail subscribers to his e-mail list. His traffic is through the roof.

His Alexa score is the best it's ever been. Look beyond where we normally think about guest posting. Set your sights higher and surprise yourself. The worst thing that can happen is they say no. If they do, move on and try again.

Your homework is to identify three big websites you have never heard of. Go to those websites and see if they accept guest posts. If they do, you know what to do.

In addition to those websites, the following large news and information websites all take contributors:

- *Huffington Post*

- The Good Men Project

- *Forbes*

- *Entrepreneur*

If you're in the marriage space, have you heard of davewillis .org? This is the website of Kimanzi's friend and in addition to having a huge e-mail list, his Facebook page has over 700,000 likes.

If you're in the career space, visit http://penelopetrunk.com. Check out the Alexa ranking at http://alexa.com/siteinfo/http:/ penelopetrunk.com.

If you're in the lifestyle design space, have you heard of seanogle (http://www.seanogle.com/)? It's another large website that most people aren't trying to guest post for.

These are just a few examples, but our goal is to open up your eyes to the possibilities. Let's all stop trying to swim in the same pond. Instead let's dive right into the ocean!

Kimanzi would have never gotten that extra 55,000 site visitors if he'd kept doing the same old, same old. That *Huffington Post* article brought in more business than Kimanzi can handle right now.

Kimanzi's goal is *not* to make you think he's some great guy. He's just a regular person who's trying to figure out what works. His goal is to show you that those of us who are building can get big opportunities if we're willing to put in the legwork.

Do you see how it works now? All you need is one big break and you can leverage that into so much more. You then have that credibility behind you. If there's something you really want to do, you can do it.

Use the power of large websites and exposure to help you build your business without chasing influencers.

Chapter 18

CALL ON YOUR AUDIENCE TO TAKE ACTION

PODCAST MOVEMENT

Podcast Movement (http://www.podcastmovement.com) is a huge testimony to the power of collaboration. We learned from Philip Taylor's experience with creating FinCon (the Financial Bloggers Conference). He was gracious enough to have a phone call with Dan Franks, Gary Leland, Mitch Todd, and Jared. He answered their questions about what he would do if he had to start FinCon again from the beginning. They were grateful to acquire this type of wisdom from Taylor, partly because he was a previous guest on Jared's podcast.

The power of that interview connection created a rapport between Taylor and Jared. He was glad to help when Jared's team had questions. Taylor would probably have helped anyway because he is a generous guy. That said, Jared has no doubt that their podcast interview connection played a small part in his willingness to say yes.

KICKSTARTER

We can't explain everything necessary in order to create a successful Kickstarter campaign in this short chapter (https://www.kickstarter.com/hello). However, we will say that Kickstarter served as an amazing way for their group to validate the idea for the Podcast Movement Conference. Kickstarter allowed them to test the market to see if creating this conference was a good idea, or not worth the time, effort, and resources.

The community voted with their wallets. We did not have an e-mail list, but we had connections within the podcasting community. Our relationships with fellow podcasters helped us to get our initial speakers, attendees, and social proof.

Dan Franks deserves tremendous credit for researching our Kickstarter campaign. He helped us come up with great rewards even though we were unable to find very many successfully funded events similar to ours. Here is the Podcast Movement Kickstarter link: https://www.kickstarter.com/projects/680579142/podcast-movement-2014-national-podcast-conference.

We needed $11,000 to book a small conference center in Addison (a small suburb of Dallas). We launched our Kickstarter campaign in February 2014, a few days before Valentine's Day. The podcast community showed up. We exceeded $11,000 after nine hours. Jeff Brown from the *Read to Lead* podcast and the Podcaster Academy (http://www.podcasteracademy.com) supported the campaign to push us over our goal!

The campaign continued for thirty days. We had over $30,000 at the end. We outgrew the small conference center and had to move to a larger hotel conference center in Dallas.

Dan, Gary, Mitch, and Jared experienced the "PT/FinCon founder" effect. The success of the Podcast Movement catapulted each of them into a higher status in the podcasting community. Jared never used to get asked to do interviews on other podcasts when he was spending countless hours working on *Starve the Doubts*. The Podcast Movement changed that. Co-founding this event has increased the visibility of his podcast and increased his audience and connections.

If you want to hear the longer version of how the conference for podcasters by podcasters was started, please consider listening to this podcast episode with Todd Cochrane, Rob Greenlee, and Dan Franks: http://www.techpodcasts.com/tms/130838/new -media-show-53-dan-franks-of-podcast-movement/.

What impact could such an event have for you and your audience? Could the perception of that event increase the visibility of your business?

Are you willing to market before you manufacture and start with a co-organized smaller event to serve your community?

IDEAS FOR FINDING A LOCATION FOR A SMALLER EVENT

Airbnb - https://airbnb.com

Pre-sell tickets and rent a mansion or larger home. Kimanzi, Gene Hammett, and Jared rented a villa in Maui for the Work Hard Play Hard Summit in 2014 (http://www.workhardplayhardsummit .com).

Your local church

Kent Julian has a great event for public speaking called Speak It Forward (http://speakitforward.com). He has events in a multipurpose room that he rents from his local church. You are welcome to tweet Kent if you have questions about events. His Twitter handle is @kentjulian.

Local college or university

Joel Zaslofsky is the founder of the SimpleREV conference (http://simplerev.com). SimpleREV was held at the University of St. Thomas campus in downtown Minneapolis.

Your home

This idea will not be for everyone. However, Dan Miller from http://48days.com has most of his events on his property in Franklin, Tennessee, which he affectionately calls "the sanctuary." Check out his Innovate event for ideas: http://www.48days .com/liveevents/inov48/.

Cruise ship

Lou Mongello puts together a community cruise every year for the "box people" (his nickname for his community). The cruise has grown and easily fills 600 spots each year. Lou uses a travel agent to help set this up. Check out the Walt Disney World Radio Community Cruise at http://www.wdwradio.com and click on Events.

One of the best resources we could leave you with is a podcast on creating events! Jared's good friend Vernon Foster has done the exhaustive research for you. Please consider checking out http:// eventsupremacy.com and send a tweet to Vernon@vernonfoster.

CHAPTER 19

SOMETIMES IT HURTS TO ASK

Let's be honest, patience is not a quality most of us are born with. As entrepreneurs, we want to grow our business, and we want to progress quickly. One strategy that has been passed around for ages is to ask for advice from successful entrepreneurs. You may have seen this in action yourself from people asking you for advice.

It can range from the "Let me pick your brain," or "I have a quick question" e-mail, to someone trying to grab a few minutes at a conference or event. It seems harmless enough, and we're told to be persistent, but asking could be hurting your chances of making a real connection with someone who could help your business.

The ask should not exceed your relationship.

Kimanzi was at a conference last year and heard a speaker explain this eloquently. She asked a guy in the audience his first name. He said it was Mike. She then said, "It's nice to meet you Mike, can I kiss you on the lips?" The crowd erupted into laughter.

She went on to say that this is what we do with relationships, and especially with other entrepreneurs. We haven't connected with them at all, yet we ask them for information they either paid to learn or took years to figure out. We are essentially asking for that kiss on the lips.

Maybe you think it's OK to ask because that's what we have always been taught to do, but if your ask exceeds the relationship, you risk alienating that entrepreneur. It might even be offensive if your first interaction is to ask for free advice. You're asking for their most valuable resource: their time. It does hurt to ask, and it could affect your chance of a future mentor, business partner, or friend.

THE RIGHT APPROACH

Successful entrepreneurs produce a wealth of free content. They have blogs, podcasts, videos, and webinars that give you clues to their success. Studying the material and implementing what they teach is hard work that turns off many entrepreneurs. It's a lot easier to ask, thinking you'll get that silver bullet to speed up your progress.

Kimanzi has experienced this personally. Since he's started writing for *Entrepreneur,* every day he gets an e-mail from some-body he doesn't know asking for an introduction to his editor. There's no interest in him or his business, or what it took for him to be writing. The e-mailers just want the quickest and easiest way to bypass the hard work.

There's a better way to connect with successful entrepreneurs. It starts with studying and applying their free content. They work hard to produce that free content, and are impressed and happy when you use it successfully. While everyone else is trying to "kiss them on the lips," you are separating yourself by showing how much you value what they do.

Use their content and share it. Thank them publicly and tell them what results you've gotten. When we say publicly, we mean social media. Successful entrepreneurs get hundreds of e-mails, and most of them are self-serving. Tweet to them. Comment on their Facebook fan page. Leave a meaningful comment on their blog. Make it brief but powerful.

Try to establish a relationship. We're not saying you have to be their best friend, but you have to build some familiarity. Don't approach influencers the way everyone else does.

YOU HAVE TO CRAWL BEFORE YOU WALK

We live in an exciting time. Today, you can be successful all on your own. There's no need to chase influencers; but if you do, just realize it takes time and work. There are no overnight successes, just entrepreneurs who do what it takes to achieve success.

It's frustrating to successful entrepreneurs when someone doesn't understand their value or how much they value their time. A successful entrepreneur's time is the most valuable and expensive part of their business.

To get access to that time, you have to pay, or pay your dues. To be successful in anything, you have to pay your dues. Don't be like everyone else looking for a shortcut. Don't ask for that kiss on the lips. Figure out what you need to do to be successful all on your own.

CHAPTER 20

SIX THINGS YOU MUST HAVE TO SUCCESSFULLY TRANSITION OUT OF YOUR DAY JOB

Entrepreneurship is not for everyone. However, if your dream is to create freedom while building financial stability, entrepreneurship can open doors that most people won't walk through.

There are those reading this that have a day job but long for a business that supports them. There are some who already are building a business on the side, and there are those who will make the transition.

Wherever you are in the process, there are six "musts" you need before you make the leap into this crazy world of entrepreneurship. If you make the move without being ready, you risk turning the dream into a nightmare. Use these six "musts" to transition out of your day job into a business that you love by the end of this year.

1. An emergency fund.

Life would be wonderful if everything went according to plan, but this isn't a movie. Your plans will get derailed. For those times, you're going to need a financial cushion to break your fall. Hope for the best, but plan for the worst. This will help ease your stress level and keep you from being one step away from a business failure. The income for entrepreneurship can be sporadic. An emergency fund will help you weather any financial storms.

2. A consistently profitable business.

There are highs and lows with any business. Too often, we only focus on the highs as proof that we're ready to transition fully to entrepreneurship. That's a recipe for disaster. Before you transition, you need a business that consistently generates income at or above your day job. That's not to say every month will be better than the last, but over a period there should be a pattern of profitability. Too many entrepreneurs have a good month and make the leap too soon.

3. A plan for growth.

A business lives or dies by its growth. You need a plan to take your business to new and higher levels of growth. You can have the best idea, and maybe even seen some progress, but you still need a plan that keeps your business growing. That growth is what helps build something that takes you out of your day job.

4. A persevering mind-set.

Sometimes you have to quit in entrepreneurship. Quitting a bad idea, the wrong marketing plan, or a part of your business that isn't profitable anymore doesn't mean failure—but having a defeated mind-set does. Successful entrepreneurs have determined that no matter what, they will do whatever it takes to reach all of their goals. Your mind-set has an effect on the action you take. The confidence from a persevering mind-set attracts customers to do business with you.

5. Thick skin.

Our society has been trained to believe that success is college and a "good job." We know that many successful entrepreneurs have proven otherwise, but most people in your life won't get it.

For years when I tried to explain what I do and the vision, it was met with polite nods. Later, I would hear that person had a different opinion that they freely expressed to others. That would bother me.

Learn to ignore the naysayers and don't bother trying to explain what you do to them. Focus on building your business and let them jump on the bandwagon once you're wildly successful. The very moment you make the transition, get ready to repel those who don't (and probably never will) understand.

6. Single-minded focus.

You're probably going to start out as a one-person show, which means large periods of time when only you are responsible for getting things done. It can be lonely, and you can become easily distracted.

At a day job, you have a boss and assignments that keep you on track. You have co-workers all around you who keep you from getting lonely or distracted.

Before you make the transition, test your focus. Make sure you won't make the transition only to spend unproductive hours that stretch into unproductive days and weeks. Discipline yourself to ignore all the bright shiny lights and to focus on the strategies that build your business.

We have begun a new year, the time to set goals and make resolutions. The stats tell us that most of these won't last past the first few months of the new year.

Whether you've made the transition or not, you're reading this because you're an entrepreneur. We think differently than the typical 9-to-5er. Having an entrepreneurial mind-set is crucial for getting started, but is not enough by itself to succeed. You have to lay a solid foundation if you are to reach your goals.

CHAPTER 21

SIX STEPS TO BECOMING A LIFESTYLE ENTREPRENEUR

The Internet has been used by academia since the 1980s, but in the past fifteen years it has become what we know today. Today, 2.5 billion people log on to the Internet every day, and it's estimated that the number will double in the next five years.

For entrepreneurs looking to start or grow a business, the Internet offers a fairly unlimited and mostly untapped customer base. There are many successful lifestyle entrepreneurs, but they are just scratching the surface of the opportunity that's available.

A "lifestyle entrepreneur" is an entrepreneur who makes their living online. They don't have a physical location or need one to operate. All they need is a laptop and connection to the Internet to manage their business. There are several tools and software they use, but they're portable.

They are not tied down, which allows them to operate their business all around the world. There can also be a passive income element to their business, but it's not necessary. If they offer services—such as coaching or consulting—they can work over Skype.

If this type of entrepreneurship model appeals to you, here are six steps you can use to becoming a location-independent lifestyle entrepreneur.

1. Pick a profitable target audience.

We're not going to give you the standard "choose your niche" advice. While being specific can help, it's not always necessary. Where niching helps is when you get industry-specific. Idea specific is a lot harder to niche.

The more important point is to make sure your "niche" or target audience can afford to pay you. Too many entrepreneurs pick a group that interests them but can't afford their products and services. You are creating a business; there has to be a potential to generate income with whatever audience you pick.

2. Build a simple foundation.

The foundation of a lifestyle entrepreneur's business is the website. A website, however, will be a constant work in progress and holds too many entrepreneurs back. You don't need all the fancy widgets and plug-ins; you don't need the best-looking website in the world. The only way your website hurts you is if it's too cluttered and confusing. Zen Habits has over a million readers, which proves simple works, as long as the content is good.

A foundation has other essential elements:

- A robust and active social media presence.

- A large emergency fund—just in case and for the slow months.

- Tools and software that help grow your business.

- Connection with your audience on a deeper level.

3. Focus on what works for you.

The Internet has given us access to success. You see successful lifestyle entrepreneurs talking about what's working for them and you're tempted to copy. Successful entrepreneurs model success. They don't copy.

You have to figure out what works for you and your business. Just because it worked for someone else, doesn't mean it will help your business. The best things you can do are to test and learn what works. It takes incredible and strategic focus to build a lifestyle business.

4. Get exposure and grow your audience.

Creating a strong social media is one great way to build your audience, but there are strategies that could get you better and "20%" results.

- *Be a guest on podcasts.* There are podcasts that get more downloads than radio stations have listeners.

- *Guest post on other blogs.* In 2012, guest posting on fifty different blogs brought 500,000 unique visitors to Kimanzi's website.

- *Write for large authority sites.* Writing for large websites such as the *Huffington Post* and *Entrepreneur* has grown Kimanzi's e-mail list from 3,000 people to over 20,000 in less than a year.

These are a few ways to get exposure and build your audience quickly. As the Internet grows, so will the effectiveness of these and other strategies.

5. Offer value and charge what you're worth.

When you provide value through your free content, people will want to dig deeper. Your paid content is what they turn to. Too many entrepreneurs don't charge based off of the value they provide.

Offer your value by consistently creating free content that's better than others' paid content. Charge a fair but profitable price for your premium offerings. Lifestyle entrepreneurs value their time above everything else, so their time is the most expensive service they offer.

6. Study what's working and scale.

Once you have made progress, review what's working for your business. See where you can make the process smoother and more efficient. Spend your time growing that profitable part of your business and scale that progress.

Focus on what's working and commit only to learn what will help your lifestyle business grow. Don't become a victim of information overload—which has crippled many entrepreneurs.

Being a lifestyle entrepreneur has been amazing for us—we enjoy real freedom. We don't want you to think it's all roses because there are real challenges. It takes years to build this kind of business, and it can be a roller coaster ride income-wise.

If this type of business appeals to you, know that it's possible and profitable. Do your homework and use these six steps to building the kind of business that best supports the type of life you want to live.

At the end of the day, this isn't about money—it's about freedom in every area of your life. When you experience this freedom, you can live life on YOUR terms.

CHAPTER 22

LOOK FOR BIGGER OPPORTUNITIES

Here we are at the last chapter. We hope you've enjoyed this journey with us. This is where it all leads. At this point we've given you a blueprint that you can use to become your own influencer.

The point is to serve your audience, to help them with their biggest struggles, and to also build a business that gets you away from a job you hate to full freedom.

If you follow our advice, you should have some leverage at this point. Get your foot in the door so you can open more doors.

We have to think bigger than what we normally think. Our goal is for this book to become a *New York Times* best seller. We're done with thinking small. You are destined for great things, and if you're going to get there, you have to believe in yourself.

In thirteenth-century Scotland there was a freedom fighter named William Wallace. You probably know about him because Mel Gibson portrayed him in the movie *Braveheart*. In a time when most people in Scotland were willing to settle, Wallace wanted more for himself and for his people.

Getting there was something that probably seemed impossible. The idea of winning freedom from a ruthless king probably seemed insurmountable.

There has been some debate about the accuracy of the movie, but one line really caught our attention. At one point the nobles ask Wallace what he'll do next, and he tells them he'll invade England. They laugh and tell him it's impossible. He then says, *"Why? Why is that impossible? You're so concerned with squabbling for the scraps from Longshank's table that you've missed your God-given right to something better."*

Wow! It may be a line from the move *Braveheart*, but it has power. Although just a line from a movie, the sad thing is that this is how most people live their lives. They're content with the scraps and completely ignore their right to a better life.

Whether it's working at a job you hate, living in a place that makes you miserable, looking at yourself in the mirror and not recognizing yourself, or a living with regret and unfulfilled dreams, the bottom line is we settle instead of soaring.

THIS IS WHO I AM: A MESSAGE FROM KIMANZI

For twelve years of my life, this was how I lived. I believed all my doubts and fears. I made every excuse in the book. I believed all those people who told me it wasn't possible. I believed the ones who told me I didn't have enough education.

I was content to just pretend instead of listening to what I knew my heart was screaming at me: don't settle!

After I woke up like William Wallace and could finally "see it," a major shift happened in my mind that led to where I am today.

I went from delivering bread at midnight for twelve years to self-publishing two e-books that sold over 86,000 copies. The second e-book was picked up by a publisher and hit bookstores this past May. I started speaking, and in the last two years spoke at conferences in twelve states and twelve countries.

I'm now completely supported by a location-independent, freedom-based online business, and on April 8, 2014, our family followed a lifelong dream and moved to Hawaii! I don't know where you are in your life right now, but I'm guessing seeing it and believing it is something that you might be dealing with.

- *Don't settle.* Life is far too short to settle. We're not guaranteed anything, and time is something we'll never get back, so why waste it on regret? Why waste it doing things we don't really want to do, living a life someone else thinks we should live?

- *Go after all those dreams and passions!* Don't hold them inside anymore! No matter where you are, no matter what's going on, you can make your dream life your real life.

- *You deserve so much more.* We are all destined for amazing things. We just never fully realize it or believe it. I know many who read this want to add value, to help people through difficult situations, and have a passion to make this a better world. You can do it!

- *You deserve to be happy.* You deserve an incredible life, but it's up to you to claim it and make it a reality.

- *Take action.* Claim the life you truly deserve.

- *At the end of the day you have to take action on your passion.* You have to chase those dreams before they can become a reality. Everywhere you look, there are stories about how New Year's resolutions don't work.

- *Yes, most people do give up, but you don't have to be most people.* The key is that I got back up and kept pushing forward. So if you set some resolutions or goals and fall down, get back up.

- *Don't listen to what others tell you about what is right for you.* Don't give them that power. Determine what *you* want to accomplish this year and go after it with everything you've got. If you fall down or get frustrated, lick your wounds, get back up, and keep pushing forward. This is *your* year!

CALL TO ACTION

We have really enjoyed having you here. We hope you got tremendous value from this book and use it to become an influencer yourself. We've given you everything you need. It's up to you.

This won't mean anything unless you get over your fear and do something about this. Here's the thing, though: there are people who will read all these words and won't do anything about it because of fear. Fear is the number-one reason many people don't chase or make big dreams their reality.

We can completely relate because we let fear hold us back. We were afraid of change, we were afraid of taking action, and we let that fear talk us out of a lot of big decisions.

Even when our businesses supported our families, we still gave in to fear. We were afraid we weren't good-enough writers so we only sent guest posts to smaller websites. We were afraid we didn't have any "credentials," so we didn't coach.

We were afraid we didn't have anything to teach or that people wouldn't take us seriously, so we didn't approach things the way we should have. We were afraid of our own shadows.

I know there are some reading this who can relate. We let our fear keep us back from going after big opportunities we can totally reach! For two years we ignored the *Huffington Post*, even though it was always a dream.

Fear is holding you back from incredible opportunities to grow your business to where it can support you. If you can't get over those fears, you'll never make your dream your reality.

FEAR IS USUALLY STUPID

Most of the time we're afraid of things we don't really need to be afraid of. If you try to do something and it doesn't work out, so what? Life continues on, and more than likely that isn't going to be your only opportunity.

Most fears are usually over dumb things that can be quickly dismissed if we step back from the situation. Yes, there are some valid concerns, but not really anything you need to be afraid of.

Stop letting fear win. Realize that everyone fails, even the "greats." The people who are successful in life have determined that no matter how many times they've failed, they're going to get back up! Be that person.

NOTHING IS IMPOSSIBLE

It may be scary and it may be outside your comfort zone to chase big dreams, but realize all of your dreams are possible.

They may not happen overnight, and it's going to take some hard work, but you can do it.

We live in an incredible time with amazing opportunities all around us. Everything you need to make your dream a reality is right in front of you. We have amazing technology that makes this all possible, especially if you have an online dream.

The message we want you to take away from this book is that if you want to build a business that supports your family, you can. More than that, it's not going to take as long as you think.

The number-one thing that has held you back to this point is fear. You may know that or it may be buried deep inside, but you have to get real with yourself. Verbalize that fear and start working on getting over it.

One of the best things we did to deal with our fear was to connect with an amazing group of friends. They were there for us as we chased huge life dreams and are the main reason our fear didn't win.

If you don't have a group like that, you need to create one or join an existing group. That support will push you past your fear and help you realize your true potential.

Our prayer is that many of you make your dreams a reality by the end of this year. We want you to land those big articles and book company contracts. We want you to do everything you think isn't possible.

Stop chasing influencers and become one yourself. You can do this.

Why? You don't want to live a life of regret!

In April 2012, Kimanzi's father died at the age of fifty-four. He was relatively young, and his death was a shock. As Kimanzi sat thinking during his funeral, he kept replaying the last few conversations they had.

The one thing he said in those conversations was that he wished he had done more. He told Kimanzi he had so many dreams and goals that he never did anything about. He told Kimanzi to learn the lesson he never learned: don't die with regret.

His death was a wake-up call and started Kimanzi on a journey where he lost 170 pounds, moved from Milwaukee to his family's dream designation of Maui. He left a job he was miserable at to follow his dream of writing.

Along the way, Kimanzi learned seven key lessons to not living a life of regret. Here are *seven choices you'll regret at the end of your life if you don't do something about them today.*

1. Not truly living.

Too often we let our doubt and fear hold us back from the amazing life we all can live. We have so many things we want to do in life yet never do. Truly living doesn't mean you're skydiving every other day. It means you don't hold back. You chase those dreams. You ignore those doubts and create that amazing life. It means that no matter how many times you fall, you get back up and keep pushing forward.

2. Not chasing your dreams.

Most people spend forty to sixty hours of their week working. When you spend that much time doing something, it will affect your life one way or another. If you're doing work that makes you miserable, every other part of your life will be affected. There are opportunities all around us, and people are making their dreams a reality as you're reading this. It's not going to be easy and it will take time, but it will be worth it.

3. Accumulating too much stuff.

When we moved to Hawaii we were shocked by how much stuff we had. We go through life getting things and saving them, and we're afraid to throw things away we don't use. Generally, if you haven't used something in the last year, you probably don't need it (there can be exceptions, of course). That stuff creates clutter, which will lead to stress. At the end of your life you won't remember any of that stuff but you will remember any incredible experiences.

4. Letting jealousy win.

Unfortunately, jealousy is part of human nature, but there are some who know how to deal with it. If you can't control jealousy, you'll definitely live a life of regret. Be grateful for your life. Be grateful that you are alive. You may not have as much as someone else, but you can and you will if you do something about it.

5. Constantly comparing yourself to other people.

As I made big changes in my life, one way I measured my progress was comparing my results to what others were doing. I learned the hard way that comparing yourself to others only leads to bitterness and heartache. Your journey is your journey and shouldn't be compared. Make changes at your own pace.

6. Letting negative people hold you back.

We're excited to tell our friends or family about changes we're making in our lives. Sometimes they're not as excited as we are and sometimes they're even negative. If you want to move forward, you have to stay away from negative people. Negative people aren't happy with themselves and will poison your progress. Pretty soon you'll start to believe what they're saying and quit. Get rid of the negative and you'll live a happier life.

7. *Starting tomorrow.*

We always think we have more time, when the reality is that we're not guaranteed a tomorrow. Every day is a gift, and we should live each day as if it were the last. The time to start isn't tomorrow, because tomorrow may never come. Start today, and tomorrow you'll be closer to living out your dream. Start today, and you won't die with regret in your heart.

I can tell you from personal experience that chasing your dreams is hard work. There are many ups and downs. There are many days when you want to quit. The best thing you can do is take it one day at a time. Instead of focusing on the big changes you want to make, focus on waking up and doing what you have to do that day. As you take it one day at a time, you'll look up after a while and realize you're there.

Life is too short to spend even a single moment miserable. Chase those dreams and create that amazing life. Come to the end of your life with a smile on your face, knowing you have no regrets.

How are you living a life of no regrets?

That's it! Thank you for sticking it out with us. Use the information in this book to create the life you truly want to live.

We created a ton of free resources to help you and that go along with this book at http://stopchasinginfluencers.com/.

Kimanzi and *Jared*

ABOUT THE AUTHORS

 **KIMANZI CONSTABLE** is a former bread delivery guy who self-published two books that have sold over 86,000 copies. In the past year he has lost 170 pounds and moved his family to Maui, Hawaii. You can usually find him writing while enjoying an ocean view. He is a published author, international speaker, and coach. He's a contributing writer to *The Huffington Post*, *Entrepreneur* magazine, and MindBodyGreen. He is a business editor at The Good Men Project. His mission is to help men and women create true freedom in life. Join him at www.KimanziConstable .com and on Facebook at Kimanzi Constable.

 **JARED EASLEY** is a genuine entrepreneur. He has been called the Zig Ziglar of the podcasting world. In the past couple of years he's started a podcast, written a book, and co-founded Podcast Movement, which is the world's largest international podcasting-only conference. Jared is a noticer, motivator, friend, and power-content creator. He has found the way to do all of this and still keep his family first.